The Royal Candlelight and You

The Royal Candlelight Presents

The Royal Candlelight and You
The Devotional Cookbook

10 Recipes for Godly Living

*Spiritual Gourmet Fine Dining Culinary Cuisines
for the
True Believer of God*

by Lynn Williams

Your Spiritual Gourmet Chef

Royal Candlelight Christian Publishing Company
"Royalty in the Making"

The Royal Candlelight 5 Book Series: The Royal Candlelight and You
© 2008 by Lynn Williams

Royal Candlelight Christian Publishing
P.O. Box 3021
Fontana, California 92334
www.royalcandlelight.com
info@royalcandlelight.com
Internet TV Website: Ustream tv.com (Royal Candlelight)

Editor: Rachel Starr Thomson
Graphic & Media Arts Designer: Talon Williams
Book Layout Designer: Lynn Williams
Sales & Marketing Director: Paul Williams
Website Designer: Ebenezer Jesutimi

ISBN-10: 0692250816
ISBN 13: 978-0692250815

Printed in the United States of America

Table of Contents

New Testament Meals

Word and Term Study
Verse-To-Verse Study
Character Study
Chapter Study *(Analysis)*
Outlining the Principal Features of the Meal
Your Daily Bread Spiritual Journal

DEDICATIONS
from
A Royal Princess

Dedication to My Beloved King
Scripture: Psalm 119:103
"How sweet are thy words to my taste!
Yes, *sweeter* than honey to my mouth!"

Thank you, my beloved King, for allowing me to dine from your blessed banquet table, where the precious Royal Candlelight, Jesus Christ shines brightly on the spiritual meals prepared from the sweetest portions of spiritual food. As I dine, I am nourished in becoming a healthy princess. You mature me into walking worthy of the calling that was placed on my life in accordance with your grace and mercy.

Dedication to Every Prince and Princess From the Spiritual Gourmet Kitchen of Your Spiritual Gourmet Chef

To every prince and princess of the royal family of God.

Scripture: Psalm 27:1
"The Lord is my *light* and my salvation; whom shall I fear?
The Lord is the defense of my life; whom shall I dread?"

We Will Make It Because the Royal Candlelight Lights The Way

We will make it, we will survive

When the enemy comes in to try to take our lives

God will step in and lift his standards

With divine protection for us because

God will not allow any weapon to form and prosper against us

We will make it by faith

Our future will be brighter than today

So praise the King

Because of the Royal Candlelight,

we will make it and we will survive.

Foreword

By

Pastor Owusu Hodari, Ph.D

Many times in our journey through this life, we as saints of the Living God encounter a work by the Holy Spirit that grabs our attention. Many books and testimonies from the children of God inspire us to reach for a higher level of comprehension of the things of God. When you encounter such a morsel of manna from heaven, it behooves you to pay attention. I have found in this book, *The Royal Candlelight and You*, such a delightful presentation of truth that I could not put it down because of the desire to see what was next. Lynn Williams has used her gift from God in the culinary arts to inspire the reader to explore the vastness of meaning of the Word of God. What a wonderful adventure Lynn leads the reader through, and at the same time she creates in the reader a desire to know more about the Word of God. The Lord Jesus reminds us in his Word that "Man does not live by bread alone, but by every word that proceeds from the mouth of God." *(Matthew 4:4)* This is important for the children of God to remember. Too often we find in our churches people who do not read or understand the Word, yet this Word is vital for our existence.

As you journey through this adventure of information and study, you will find that Lynn has a unique ability to help you to focus on ways to remember the Scriptures. Lynn has provided the reader with a study guide that involves the reader in delving into the meaning and understanding of the Scriptures. This study guide also provides culinary delights that you can literally taste as you continue on your journey. What a wonderful way to learn and discuss the Word of God!

Chapter 1

Meal Presentation

Scripture: James 1:17
"_Every good thing_ bestowed
and every _perfect gift_ is from above,
coming down from the Father of _lights_,
with whom there is _no variation_ or shifting shadow."

Meal Presentation

The Royal Candlelight and You is a spiritual recipe book from a five-book series of spiritual cuisines at their best. You can classify the recipes in this book as gourmet fine dining because the meals are especially prepared for you to focus on the Royal Candlelight, Jesus Christ, and some of his characteristics and attributes. There is no finer food for the soul and spirit! This collection of fine dining includes in-depth studies of ten specially selected "meals" (books) from the New Testament, each prepared to cast a bright light on the sweetness of the love, grace, and sacrifices of our Lord and Savior, Jesus Christ. The Royal Candlelight shines so that you can see the purpose of his birth, life, death, and resurrection. Each section uses biblical lessons prepared by the Master Chef's assistants, the sous chefs (apostles, prophets, evangelists, pastors, and teachers), under the direction and spiritual guidance of the Master Chef, Jesus Christ. The spiritual sous (pronounced "sue") chefs made significant contributions, which included simplifying each menu in accordance with the principles of the gospel.

The spiritual gourmet meals found in this book include a special feast presented as four courses of great spiritual home cooked meals that are served to you individually from the King's banqueting table, the Bible. The meal studies are structured so that you can spend valuable time at the royal dinner table studying the Word of God as you dine on the various courses, gaining a working knowledge of the Royal Candlelight and you as you do. Each meal is going to take a great deal of precious time to eat because of the amount of spiritual food served in each course. You will have the opportunity to experience and enjoy each course as it is plated and served to you. The King has picked up the tab for these gourmet cuisines—he just wants you to pick up the tip by spending time with him, so that this gourmet fine dining experience will be worth the cost because the money you spend on these ten sweet-tasting spiritual meals will guaranteed to richly fill you up with spiritual knowledge and eliminate any shadows of doubt about the Royal Candlelight.

Please take your time dining on each course so you don't become miserable and frustrated from eating too much at one time without knowing what you have eaten. This will also keep you from getting discouraged and developing spiritual indigestion because you haven't thoroughly chewed (meditated on) your spiritual food and satisfied your heart with gladness.

The particular ten gourmet meals in this book have been chosen to allow you to master the general contents of ten books of the Bible designed to enlighten you about Jesus, the *Lamb* of God, while learning about who *you* are as his sheep. Questions have been provided after each lesson to help stimulate your thinking as well as contribute to your spiritual maturity.

The Royal Candlelight and You will heighten your knowledge of God and provide a more in-depth, thorough understanding of the raw "food" material used by the Master Chef, Jesus Christ, in his great recipe book for all of life — the Bible.

This book has been written as a culinary allegory to demonstrate and express great truths using the familiar images of dining techniques and cuisines. Its objective is to vividly communicate the truth of Scripture by providing the royal family of God with allegories that can be used to increase our interest in learning the real truth about God, his only begotten Son, and the life he calls us to conduct as the King's children under the guidance of the Holy Spirit.

The Royal Candlelight lights the way for you to walk worthy of your calling. However, the key to walking worthy is obedience so you can stay in step with God as you walk on the path where his light shines. In order for you to walk worthy of your calling, God expects you to embrace your salvation by helping those who are less fortunate, performing the good works he has prepared for you as his disciples. We are to express our faith in our love for God and for one another through our humility, meekness (gentleness), longsuffering (patience), tolerance, endurance, peace, and unity with each other. These seven saving graces complete a walk worthy enough to please God in all aspects. Living in this way will produce fruit in every good work and increase your knowledge of God. We are to be examples by our convictions, no matter who or what opposes them. We should never compromise our trust, faith, or belief in Jesus Christ. Our bodies, our spirits, our hope, our Lord, our faith, our baptism, and our God and Father are all based on the foundational truth of what we believe.

Our bodies are all members of the body of Christ that was created by the Holy Spirit of God. *Our spirits* are indwelled by the same Holy Spirit who indwells every believer, and we all belong to each other in the Lord. *Our hope* is in the return of the Lord to take us, his church, to heaven. *Our Lord* is Jesus Christ, who died for us. *Our faith* is in the Son of God, who delivered us. *Our baptism* of the Holy Spirit is where he has placed the believing sinner into the body of Christ, and *our relationship with our God and Father* who is over us, through us, and in us is based on our acceptance of his Son, our Lord, which gives us the privilege of calling our God "Father." This causes all of us to walk together in unity.

This recipe book is suited for Bible study classes as well as independent or group study. I pray that you will not be considered one of those whom the Lord said would perish due to lack of knowledge. *(Hosea 4:6)* Its dishes have been prepared with some of the finest spiritual spices of love, sweet herbs of compassion, and other spiritual ingredients to satisfy every prince and princess's fine dining pleasures.

Chapter 2

The Royal Candlelight...

Scripture: John 8:12
"...I am the <u>light</u> of the <u>world</u>; he who <u>follows</u> Me shall not walk in the <u>darkness</u>,
but shall have the <u>light of life</u>." (NASB)

The Royal Candlelight...

The Royal Candlelight and You lessons focus on Jesus as the Messiah, as foretold by the Old Testament prophets. As you feast, you will come across names and terms such as *kingdom of heaven, God's only begotten Son, Son of Man,* and *Son of God.* You will be introduced to Jesus's discourses, especially the Sermon on the Mount and his discussion of his Second Coming and what's to come at the end of the world.

Names in the Bible, especially in the Old Testament, were often an indication of a person's character or particular qualities. The same is true regarding Jesus's names. His names will reveal his character and special qualities as he deals with mankind. His names will also clearly indicate the creative and divine governing powers of his sovereignty. The Royal Candlelight's many roles and functions will be described under these various names, such as *Jesus, the Messiah, the Christ,* and the *Anointed One.* You will learn that Jesus is his personal name, while "Messiah" or "Christ" is his official names. From his names, you will come face-to-face with the knowledge of who Jesus is in all of his glory. It is in the face of Jesus Christ that we will best see the glory of God the Father, because in John 10:30 Jesus declares, *"The Father and I are one"*

We will come to know about the Person of God as his names are revealed in these spiritual gourmet meals. His names will not only tell us about his character, but they will also reveal his ways. We will find blessings and comfort in his names, which will signify his supreme sovereignty, glory, and great power because his name is holy and is above every name (*Psalm 91:14b: "...I will set him securely on high, because he has known My name." - NASB*)

You will discover the King's wonderful flavors of sweet love, precious grace, and tender mercy, all found in the Lamb of God, in these ten spiritual gourmet meals. You will learn about the genealogy of Jesus that validates his line of descent from the family of David, nurtured by God to become the family in which *the Promise* was fulfilled. The coming of Christ to earth as our Savior was anticipated from the very beginning of time, and his earthly family is comprised of forty-two generations of three groups of fourteen each, covering two thousand years.

From a royal point of view, as a child of the King, you will see and experience the expression of God's own holiness while he operates in eternity to reveal his eternal promise for us, his people, along with his authority, his mighty works, and his awesome acts of kindness toward us. His triumphal Second Coming will be displayed in a cloud with power and in the glory of the Father as Jesus makes his victorious grand entrance and arrives with his holy angels. You will get a close view of the Royal Candlelight's last supper, the cup, the Passover, the Lord's Prayer, the cross, the crucifixion, and the resurrection. You will also explore the marvelous teaching ministry of this Great Teacher that will include great miracles, great healings, and great teachings through parables, all of which cast great illumination on his great powers and the great love he has for us.

On the other hand, from the world's point of view, you will see the foolish reasoning and actions against the Royal Candlelight as he is disbelieved and rejected by rulers, betrayed by a friend for thirty pieces of silver, and given vinegar and gall to drink. Lots will be cast for his garments and his side will be pierced, but not a bone will be broken. He will die with transgressors and be buried in the tomb that was bought and offered to the slain Lamb of God by a rich man. He will rise from the dead on the third day and appear before many as the Risen Savior. During this spiritual event, our Savior will gain possession of the keys to Death and Hades to unlock the doors to eternal life and open heaven's gates for us to rise up so we can enter into his gates with thanksgiving and his courts with great praise.

The complete story of Jesus's life from the standpoint of the Royal Candlelight himself will shine a bright light on all the main features, incidents, and events that were foretold in detail in the Old Testament Scriptures and then come to pass in the New Testament Scriptures. The Gospel of John will describe how everything began from the Word and his deity becoming flesh. John will also tell us about how Jesus reached down into our darkness to draw us into the marvelous True Light, which has come into the world to enlighten every man. In the light, you will see more clearly the things that you could not see in the dark, especially those things that could harm you if you had remained there. The light will shine brightly on the anointing of the Son of God when Jesus is baptized, and the Holy Spirit will be seen publicly, descending like a dove as God announces his pleasure in his Beloved Son. It's all here for you to digest when you dine on these spiritual gourmet meals.

You will dine alongside of God's only begotten Son, Christ Jesus, as he reveals how he fasted for forty days and was tempted by Satan in the wilderness. The Holy Spirit, the angels, and Satan all played an important role in this great spiritual event. The Holy Spirit, who indwelled the Author and Finisher of our faith, will guide the Son of Man into the wilderness as Satan makes a failed attempt to turn him from his mission here on earth. You will taste how the angels contributed to the life of Jesus by ministering to him as they served and cared for his needs. Christ Jesus knew way back in eternity that he was coming into the world to suffer as the Lamb of God in order to save us from human sin.

The book of Hebrews will confirm that the Royal Candlelight is our High Priest forever according to the order of Melchizedek. The Great Intercessor intercedes on our behalf and is able to save forever those who draw near to the King through the Royal Candlelight, since he always lives to make intercession for us *(Hebrews 7:25)*. The Lord Jesus Christ, who is the Lamb slain from the foundation of the world, being the First and the Last, is the eternally begotten Son of God who shared God's glory before the world was spoken into existence.

In these spiritual gourmet meals, you will discover that you have a covenant relationship with an unchanging God who remains faithful forever, enabling us to put all our trust in the only true and faithful Lord of lords, because upon the Lord's faithfulness rests all of our hope and faith in his willingness to help us. You will know undoubtedly, for a fact, that Jesus is the only Way to get through to the King.

The God you will get to know in these pages is the only God of holiness, love, grace, mercy, justice, and righteousness, with perfect spiritual and moral attributes. The Great Love of our life loves us with an everlasting love because it is his very nature to love. While his *holiness* must condemn sin, our Redeemer's powerful *love* redeems us as sinners to bring us back with *grace* and *mercy* into a close and intimate relationship that represents a *just* and *righteous* fellowship with himself. The Great Love *serves* because he came not to be served, but to serve. The Great Love *gives* because he gave his own life by dying on the cross to save us from eternal damnation. The Great Love *forgives* because while on the cross, he forgave us and pardoned all of our sins. The Great Love *protects* because the Lord keeps all those who love him. The Great Love *reciprocates* because he loves those who love him, and those who diligently seek him will find him. The Great Love *promises* because he will never desert us, nor will he ever forsake us. The Great Love *comforts* because he will be with us always. But the Great Love has a question to ask you: do you have a great love for him? If so, then you will love him with all your heart, mind, soul, body and strength. If you really and greatly love him, you will also keep his commandments. The above are the most powerful ways that God has demonstrated his great love for us to lead and feed us, his sheep, through the spiritual meals found in his Word. We have found a true Friend in high places, and this true Friend sticks closer than a brother. His friendship will last a lifetime.

The All-Sufficient One is able to do exceedingly, abundantly above all that you can ever ask or think. Since he is self-sufficient, you will learn that without him you can do nothing on your own *(John 15:5)*, but through him, you can do all things because he strengthens you *(Philippians 4:13)*. The All-Abounding One in all of his extraordinary goodness chastens those he loves and purges us to bring forth much multiplying good fruit.

The book of Revelation will reveal and testify of the Almighty pouring out judgment, but also pouring forth blessings through the outpouring of our First Love. The Lamb will open the seals to pour out the judgment of sin and death on all those who reject him. The blessings, however, will be poured forth on all those who will receive the fullness of the love, grace, mercy, and eternal life of God.

In Revelation, we learn anew that God provided for

himself the Perfect Lamb who was not spotted or blemished by sin to be a living sacrifice, because "God so loved the world that He gave His Only Begotten Son" so that we might live through him and with him forever (John 3:16).

The Lord God protects, provides, and sustains his princes and princesses, who are also his servants, as he bestows upon them spiritual gifts from the Holy Spirit to equip them for service in his mighty kingdom. Jesus's parables will teach us his requirements for his servants, and the gospels of Matthew and Luke will shed light on the rewards of those servants who are faithful and obedient to the King while also explaining the consequences or punishment of those who lack faithfulness and show disobedience toward the King. The Son of Man has given his life as a ransom for many. As the Perfect Servant, he suffered to be the perfect example of how we are to serve others as servants of the Lord.

These spiritual gourmet meals will serve up understanding of the Lord as a *Fortress,* a *Deliverer,* and a *Rock.* The book of 2 Corinthians will show the Royal Candlelight opening doors that no man can shut and closing doors that no man can open. He preaches deliverance to the captives, protects the weak, gives sight to the blind, heals the sick, and raises the dead. In Matthew 16:18, the Rock reminds us that we should know *who we are* as "little rocks." We should know *where we stand,* which is on a large Rock that cannot be shaken. This Rock is no longer an object, but a Person, the Word, Christ Jesus. We should know *what we are up against.* Even though we may be up against the gates of hell, they will not prevail against us because we are strong little rocks standing upon the Living Stone, who is also called our Chief Cornerstone.

The beauty of the Lord is especially seen in his holiness because it is the one attribute that governs all of his other attributes. It is what separates him from everyone else because he is the only Holy One of God; *even his name is holy* (Luke 4:34).

Jesus is also the Prince of Peace, who is the only Anointed One who has the ability and authority to offer perfect peace to all those who surrender to his will *(John 16:33).* We are to let this same peace of God rule our hearts so that we might find perfect rest in him.

The Lord is our Shepherd, and we shall not want, because the Great Shepherd meets our every need according to his riches in glory as he leads his sheep in the direction they should go. He has equipped us in every good thing to do his will, to work in us that which is pleasing in his sight. The

Good Shepherd also took our place and laid down his life for his sheep because he knows, loves, and cares for every one of them (John 10:11).

During these ten spiritual gourmet meals the Royal Candlelight will shine brightly, so get ready to be enlightened as you sumptuously feast on the royal knowledge of the Royal Priest. I encourage you to spiritually eat all you can by filling up on this feast that will strengthen the royal blood flowing through your spiritual body. Remember, this is all about *the Royal Candlelight . . .*

Chapter 3

...and You

Prince and Princess

Scripture: Ephesians 5: 8 & 10
"For you were formerly <u>darkness</u>, but now you are <u>light</u> in the Lord;
walk as <u>Children of light</u>...trying to learn what is <u>pleasing</u> to the Lord."

...and You
Prince and Princess

The recipes in the Great Recipe Book, the Bible, have been prepared especially for every prince and princess of the kingdom of God. There is royalty imparted to the soul of a saint, which leads to receiving great advantages in being a child of the King. We receive all of the *promises* and the *blessings* that come with our royal position as we go about our royal servant duties in the kingdom to please the King. We are a ROYAL PRIESTHOOD and a HOLY NATION *(1 Peter 2:9)*, with a great responsibility and a beautiful inheritance. We have an eternal purpose: to declare with our lips the glory of God. We are to display ourselves in a way that we can make it known that we are in Christ, so that Satan, his demons, and the world will know who we are and will also know who God is in all his glory through us. We are to clearly demonstrate with our freedom and confidence that what we have declared and displayed is real and true, and that is Christ Jesus. We can draw others to the light that shines in us because we are plugged into the power source according to the King's eternal purpose, which he accomplished in Christ.

However, we first have to admit the truth about ourselves, realize some important facts, and *make some major changes.* Change does not take place if we maintain our old ways. In order to get welfare, you must first admit you are poor; to file bankruptcy, you must first admit you are broke; to be admitted to a hospital, you must first admit you are sick; and to be saved, you must first admit you were hell-bound and need a Savior. Human beings are creatures of habit, whether good or bad. As a child of the King, you need to focus on and evaluate *your new position in Christ as a new creature.* To do this, you must first *realize* your new identity – "Who am I?" Next, *renew* or change your thought life and get rid of your stinking thinking – "As a new creature, what should I now be thinking about?" Then, *recognize* that your old life (the old man or woman) is dead and buried, never to rise again – "Can I still go back to my old ways of doing things?" Now, *release* and change your bad habits – "Do I still enjoy those things that are now conflicting to the new man (or woman)?" Finally, *replace* old bad habits with new good ones – "What things can I do now that will bring God glory?"

Since your new royal position causes you to receive blessings from the King, you must *realize that your conduct and conversation through your attitude must change* by giving God praises that should immediately follow these blessings. We have obtained the riches found in Romans 2:4: the riches of his goodness, forbearing, longsuffering, grace, mercy, and loving-kindness, as well as his glory. As you dine, you will digest these riches through the richness of the Beatitudes *(Matthew 5:3–12)*. The blessings and the rewards in this powerful message were promised by the Savior and given to the lowly, discouraged, spiritually depressed, merciful, pure in heart, peaceful, and persecuted. Are you really ready for these types of rich blessings? You see, the Beatitudes are intended to "be attitudes" that God will bless if we conduct ourselves properly according to the King's measurements of our attitudes.

Matthew 5:3 — "Blessed are the *poor in spirit*, for theirs is the kingdom of heaven." The poor in spirit are deeply aware of their spiritual poverty. They look at their lack of spiritual assets and realize that they need to be rich in spirit, not by looking at themselves and what they desire, but by looking at the King who is in total control and owns everything. The kingdom of heaven is in you, and your attitude should allow God to reign and rule over the life that you have surrendered to him by crowning him King in your heart and allowing him to remain on the throne of your life.

Matthew 5:4 – "Blessed are those who *mourn*, for they will be comforted." God expects you to have an attitude that mourns over your sin to bring you to an attitude of repentance. Unfortunately, some of us have yet to learn to mourn in this way. Some of the King's kids just regret they got caught in the act of sin, but they are not truly sorrowful for sinning against God. Our sinful acts continue to break God's heart when we commit them. David said that "against You [God] and You only, I have sinned." *(Psalm 51:4)* We should come to hate sin (not the sinner) like God hates sin. To hate sin means you realize you hate what is done against God. That which grieves him should also grieve you to a point of repentance. Those who do mourn this way will be blessed not because they can cover up their sin with leaves of excuses, but because they will have an attitude that sorrows not only over their personal sin against God, but all types of sin and their repercussions, ethical and moral.

Matthew 5:5 – "Blessed are the *meek*, for they will inherit the earth." Those who display an attitude of humbleness, patience, gentleness, and kindness, God said will inherit the earth. Their inheritance will not come from their desire to get involved in get-rich-quick schemes to prosper financially or gamble away that which God has blessed them with. They will realize where their blessings come from and choose to have an attitude to *wait* on the Lord for their provisions because they shall inherit the earth.

Matthew 5:6 — "Blessed are those who *hunger and thirst* for righteousness, for they will be filled."** You should experience the depths of being spiritually hungry and thirsty after God's righteousness the same way you hunger and thirst after physical things. Those of us who fill up with this attitude realize the need to be filled with the righteousness of Christ and will thoroughly be satisfied with God's righteousness that comes from the only true Bread and Water of Life.

Matthew 5:7 — "Blessed are the *merciful,* for they will be shown mercy."** You will reap what you sow. If you show mercy, then you shall also reap mercy, which comes from having an attitude of kindness, tenderheartedness, and forgiveness toward one another even as God has toward you. The same measure you give to others will be given back to you, so be very careful not to judge others at a higher standard

THE ROYAL CANDLELIGHT AND YOU

10 Recipes for Godly Living

than you would like others to judge you. There are those who realize they are desperately in need of God's mercy every day. Those who don't receive his mercy will receive his wrath and discipline.

Matthew 5:8 — "Blessed are the *pure in heart,* **for they will see God."** Be careful about your attitude when you look at the outward appearances of others and judge them by your standards. You can't always tell who God's child is just by looking at them and judging them by the color of their skin or the type of clothes they wear. God looks at the heart, and he tells us that our heart is naturally wicked and evil; there are those who realize they need to ask God for a clean and pure heart in order to see him in the natural as they carry the right attitude in their hearts for others regardless of how they look.

Matthew 5:9 — "Blessed are the *peacemakers,* **for they will be called sons of God."** Jesus came so that he could create peace between the King and us. Before he came, we were enemies of God, and Jesus wanted to reconcile us back to a right relationship. We were at war with God and disconnected simply by the things we did against him. Jesus made peace with us, as recorded in Romans 5: while we were yet sinners and still God's enemies, Jesus died for us to reconnect us back to our heavenly Father. Now when we make peace with our own enemies, we can be considered God's peacemakers because we look more like our heavenly Father when our attitudes toward others are peaceful.

Matthew 5:10–12 — "Blessed are those who are *persecuted* because of righteousness, for theirs is the kingdom of heaven. Blessed are you when people insult you, persecute you, and *falsely say all kinds of evil* against you because of me. Rejoice and be glad, because great is your reward in heaven." Those who have a joyful attitude when they are persecuted and insulted for God's sake will rejoice when this happens because they realize they are a part of the kingdom and have rewards coming to them based on their attitudes. This shows that they are representing the kingdom of God by doing things right according to God's standards, and he is going to bless them for having a willingly joyful attitude to suffer for his sake.

As you reflect the glow from the Royal Candlelight, who is the Light of the world, you will *realize you will be enlightened and seasoned in knowledge* with enough spiritual nourishment to become the light of the world and the salt of the earth. Although you will likely not have the privilege of receiving the same facial glow that Moses did when he sat face-to-face in the presence of God to receive instructions, yet, everyone should be able to see a special glow in the face of every believer who personally experiences the presence of the King after sitting at the royal dinner table and then demonstrates what they've learned through their good deeds. We are raised up to be witnesses with a testimony, to tell the world about the Glorious Light of the world. Some in the world will only experience God's light and his glory through us as we shine from our great dining experiences, expressing our gourmet knowledge, spreading his flavorful salt, and shining this bright light of ours on the discouraged, unsaved, unchurched, and all those who are in darkness.

While dining, you will *realize, as royalty, how you are to deal with others* as you gain an appreciation for heavenly things when you focus your attention on things above. The heavenly teachings will be realized when you learn about prayer, fasting, the Narrow Way, and your purpose in life. We have been *chosen*, *predestined* and *placed* under moral obligations, with warnings of punishment or consequences if we choose to be disobedient to the King. Disobedience cancels out any blessings you were to receive from the King. When you choose to harden your heart and turn away from God by turning your attention on earthly things and placing them above the King, there is real loss. Our first obligation to the King is to love him with all our heart, mind, soul, and strength. You can't serve two masters—you will love one and hate the other. We are also expected to be *holy*, for the King is holy. Our holiness is required because of our royal position in Christ, which requires us to practice our holiness through our moral character as we represent the image of God.

Holiness has been designated as our way of life because God's divine power has given us all things that pertain to life and godliness through a true knowledge of Him. *(2 Peter 1:3)* The King demands holiness, justice, and righteousness from all those who are made in his holy image and are *called* or *anointed* according to his purpose and pleasure. We are to present our bodies as a *living sacrifice,* holy and acceptable unto God. *(Romans 12:1)* We are *washed* and *sanctified* in the holy name of our Lord and Savior, Jesus Christ, by the Holy Spirit from our Holy Father, who is in heaven.

You will *realize your fruitfulness* after applying what you have learned from spending time dining on these spiritual meals. You will gain nutritional knowledge when you acquire wisdom as "fruit inspectors" to examine the good and bad fruits of men as you discern the false teachings that are presently going forward daily from those who sit in the presence of Satan, the father of lies, and who are sent out to try to deceive you with their rotten fruits of heresies.

The Royal Candlelight sheds great light on the love that the Father has for his Son. The Son also has that same love for us, and we can abide securely in that love. That love is brilliantly reflected in his death on the cross for our sins. Those who believe in the Royal Candlelight will receive forgiveness of their sins through his name. Our salvation is guaranteed through the Risen Savior.

The Royal Candlelight faithfully shines his light to show us the evidence that gives us hope in our faith and trust in the King, but our faith should be genuine and sincere, without hypocrisy. Our faith needs to be influential to honor God as we do well and influence those around us so they will have the same faith we have in Christ. This will prove that our faith can be hereditary, because that which dwells in us will dwell in others also. God will bless those who live by faith because they have faith in things not seen, searching for the evidence that is heard and seen regarding the things hoped for when their faith is tested. Every prince and princess of the King is faithfully given the promise of eternal life, never to perish, but to be changed in the twinkling of an eye at the Last Trumpet from corruptible to incorruptible, only to put on a robe of immortality that will last forever. God operates out of eternity, so no one ever has or will have the ability to snatch us out of the hands of our King; not even Satan himself.

We are given *peace* from the King through the Royal Candlelight so that our hearts will not be troubled or fearful at the disturbances of Satan, our spiritual enemy and adversary. This peace will keep us firmly planted in the perfect will of the King and give us peace within our hearts.

The Royal Candlelight provides the fullness of bright joy, which he places in us through the things that are spoken to us in the Master Chef's spiritual meals. When we take a look at the Royal Candlelight, our hearts will rejoice greatly, and no one should be able to take this joy away from us. You will *realize the JOY* that comes from putting *Jesus* first, *Others* second, and *You* last.

We have been given freedom from the slavery of sin because where the Spirit of the Lord is, there is liberty. We were found not guilty for our sins because the Lord's death on the cross released us and set us free from the death penalty caused by our sins through the shedding of his blood, and we are by faith justified and made righteous in Christ.

As a royal child of the King, you will *realize your greatness and excellence* as it is found when you serve God and others by imitating the Greatest One of All. In his excellence, Jesus came not to be served, but to serve. He gave his Life a ransom for many. We can expect great things from God as we attempt great things for God. As his children, we are not only to minister to God by serving others, but by serving up great and excellent praises to the only wise and awesome God, our Lord and Savior. We can also minister to the King by asking him daily what he would have us to do for him that would truly please him as a loving child would bless his or her loving Father.

From the fullness of God we receive the blessings of grace upon grace, and we receive the blessings of life abundantly because God causes all things to work together for good to those who love him and who are called according to his purpose. One of our blessings includes spiritual gifts to empower us to fulfill our royal purpose for the King.

We are also blessed by the Lord's presence, for where two or three have gathered together in his name, he promises to be in their midst. He also promised to be with us always, even to the end of the ages, never to leave us nor forsake us. You will come to *realize that all of his promises are true*. After dining on these spiritual gourmet meals, you will be convinced that neither death, nor life, nor angels, nor principalities, nor things present, nor things to come, nor powers, nor height, nor depth, nor any other created thing shall be able to separate you from the love of God, which is in our Lord and Savior, Jesus Christ (Romans 8:38–39).

You will *realize the importance of prayer.* We are encouraged to pray because if we ask, it shall be given to us; if we seek, we shall find; and if we knock, it shall be opened to us. God hears his children's cries and attends to them by answering their prayers according to his will. Our heavenly Father is just a prayer away, and all our help comes from the Lord. The King gives good gifts to his children who ask, but the things you ask in prayer, you must believe in order to receive according to God's perfect will and timing. It is God's desire that we pray without doubting or ceasing. If you have any doubts, pray and ask God to help your unbelief. He also has a great desire through the Holy Spirit to talk to us in the quietness of our hearts; for we are to always pray about everything and not lose heart. It's amazing that our prayers can move the very heart of God when we come to him with faith and expectation for him to counsel us in the direction and decisions he would have us make as obedient children.

Matthew 18:19 tells us that if two of us agree on earth concerning anything that we ask, it will be done for us by our Father, who is in heaven. First John 3:22 tells us that whatever we ask, we receive from him, if we keep his commandments.

Finally, you will *realize you have the promise of Christ's return to receive you* after he has prepared estate mansions filled with many dwelling places in the King's palace for you to dwell with him forever (hallelujah and amen!).

We are arrayed in a very *special armor of greatness* because the King's desire is forever toward us. This is why it is so important to remember to stay fully dressed and suited up at all times in your royal attire of the full armor of God. Listed in Ephesians 6, these are essentially expensive spiritual garments, handmade of faith and love, to be worn by every prince and princess in the royal kingdom of the King. This six-piece designer outfit includes the Helmet of Salvation, the Breastplate of Righteous, the Shield of Faith, the Belt of Truth, the Sword of the Spirit, and Shoes of the Readiness of the Gospel. It was personally designed by the King to assist in you being properly dressed from head to toe, to face the evils and the Evil One of this world. The spiritual gourmet meals you will dine on will prepare you for blessings and the conditions to acquire them, as well as teaching you how to wear these royal garments by preparing you spiritually to deal with your human struggles against evil spirits, the fallen angels of the devil, and unclean seducing spirits, which come under Satan's organization of principalities, powers, rulers of darkness, and spiritual hosts of wickedness.

Don't forget to drink a full glass of the Aged Royal Wine, the Holy Spirit, everyday to keep you well-nourished and able to function at your fullest potential each day. The Master Chef, Jesus Christ, has requested that the King serve us this wine to be in and with us forever so that he can comfort, guide, protect, direct, counsel, instruct, prompt, warn, and assist us in every good work. You should pray and ask the Master Chef to fill you with the contents of all nine fruits of the Spirit, which are love, joy, peace, patience (longsuffering), kindness, goodness, faithfulness, gentleness, and self-control (Galatians 5:22–23). This "special fruit drink" is essential so you can walk in the Spirit and not fulfill the "passion fruits" of the desires of the flesh. The evidence of drinking this fleshly passion fruit is seen in the practice of immorality, impurity, sensuality, idolatry, sorcery, enmities, strife, jealousy, outbursts of anger, disputes, dissensions, factions, envy, drunkenness, carousing, and things like these (Galatians 5:19–21). As Christ's offspring, we are not to practice any of these behaviors if we consider ourselves princes and princesses in the kingdom of God.

Chapter 4

The Culinary Artistry of the Spiritual Sous Chefs

Scripture: Matthew 10:24; 26
"A _disciple_ is not above his _teacher_,
nor a slave above his master."
"Therefore _do not fear_ them, for there is nothing _covered_
that will not be _revealed_, and
hidden that will not be known."

The Culinary Artistry of the Spiritual Sous Chefs

The spiritual sous chefs (apostles, prophets, evangelists, pastors, and teachers – Ephesians 4:11) who were used of the Holy Spirit to write the Bible and equip the saints were completely under the divine control of God himself. These sous chefs were personally selected by the Master Chef, Jesus Christ, from various parts of the world with expertise from different cultural backgrounds and inspired to assist in presenting the greatest feast known to mankind. The position of sous chef was most demanding, with a great responsibility for the preparation of the spiritual items in every meal. They exemplified remarkable skills and commitment as they dedicated their lives to the innovation of the Highest Order.

The ten meals listed in this recipe book were prepared by the following sous chefs, and a brief description of their background and experience in preparing the meals for the Master Chef are as follows:

Sous Chef Matthew—One of the original twelve disciples, who forsook everything to follow the Master Chef, Jesus Christ. He prepared the first gospel meal found among our New Testament meals, with a message of the coming Messiah, the King of the Jews, and the kingdom of heaven.

Sous Chef Mark—The son of Mary, cousin of Barnabas, and companion of Simon Peter. He accompanied Paul and Barnabas to Antioch on their first missionary journey, but later turned back. He prepared the second gospel meal found in the New Testament, with a message as to how we as servants of God are to serve others who are less fortunate than ourselves. He presented Jesus as the Worker and the Servant. Mark takes you on a ministry tour of Jesus's activities.

Sous Chef Luke—A first-century Gentile Christian, the Beloved Physician," and the Apostle Paul's "fellow worker" because he was a close companion of Paul during his missionary journeys. As an experienced physician, knowing the physical body and how it operates, Luke prepared the third gospel meal found in the New Testament to display the humanity of Jesus as the Perfect Man by showing Jesus's loving-kindness towards the weak, the suffering, and the outcast. Luke prepared another meal in this spiritual recipe book to show how the Son of Man came in the flesh to seek and to save the lost as he expressed the formation and spreading of the church, the extension of the gospel to the Gentiles, and the life and work of the apostle Paul. He is believed to be the only Gentile writer of the New Testament.

Sous Chef John— An apostle of Jesus and the cousin and disciple of John the Baptist. He was one of the first of the twelve disciples. He prepared the fourth gospel meal found in the New Testament. This meal was prepared to give an account of Jesus's life as the Son of God. He also prepared another meal in this spiritual recipe book to reveal the future and the things to come by charting the course and destiny of the church.

Sous Chef Paul— An apostle and servant of the Master Chef, Jesus Christ. He prepared four of the spiritual meals that were selected for this recipe book. The first spiritual meal was prepared to explain the justification of our righteousness. The second was prepared to show the importance of love and the powerful force it has because it is the very essence of God's nature. The third was prepared to deal with some very serious problems and disorders that had risen in one of the churches concerning idol worship practices, the abuse of the Lord's

Supper, marital problems, and disorderly conduct in the assembling of the saints.

The fourth spiritual meal was prepared to show how Jesus became a "better sacrifice" in order to intercede for every child of God as their High Priest. You will taste and see how Jesus became the only true and living sacrifice that was sufficient for our salvation.

THE FOUR GOSPEL MEALS

Matthew, Mark, Luke, and John make up the four gospel meals in the Great Recipe Book. They can be considered the most important meals in the Recipe Book because they give us the complete account of Christ's life here on earth. The King had a hand in the preparation and preservation of these special, flavorful gospel meals, to reveal and contain what he wanted us to know about his precious Son. They were so important to the King that he used the same main ingredient, *lamb,* and the same basic recipe in all four, but he added slight variations of other spiritual ingredients to feed various churches and individuals based on their spiritual nutritional needs.

Some of these variations are found when only Matthew

and Luke tell about the birth and childhood of Jesus, but each sous chef focuses on different ingredients of the same incidents.

All four gospels meals discuss Jesus's Galilean Ministry, but Sous Chef John is the only one who discusses the early Judean ministry of Jesus and his visits to Samaria and Jerusalem. John also records the preincarnation existence of Jesus.

The gospels of Sous Chefs Matthew, Mark, and Luke are called the Synoptic Gospels because they concentrate on recording the same events and have the same point of view with regard to Jesus's life. Sous Chef John deals more with the spiritual meaning of what Jesus said and did during his stay here on earth, which supplements the other gospels. Sous Chef John strongly emphasizes the signs and wonderful miracles of Jesus to prove that Jesus is the Christ. He devotes *seven* complete chapters, which equals one-third of his gospel, to the crucifixion day from sunset to sunset.

All four gospel meals give a full account of the last week of Jesus's life here on earth, and all four sous chefs talk about Jesus's post resurrection ministry.

Chapter 5

Spiritual Fine Dining

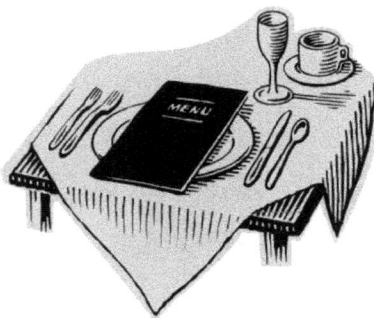

Scripture: Matthew 22:2
"The <u>kingdom</u> of heaven may be compared to a king,
who gave a <u>wedding feast</u> for his son."

Spiritual Fine Dining

Special Spiritual Treats

Special spiritual treats are listed below to teach you various ways to study the Word of God. This is where you record all those bites of information that you have gathered from your dining experiences and that you will capture on the Study Forms. This will help you in retaining your studies and can improve your appetite to start eating more and getting more spiritual food into your system in order to achieve the growth you need to mature into a healthy Christian.

Special Spiritual Treats of Meals: Study the Bible by Books

Some spiritual meals will take longer to dine on than others. You can start off by choosing a meal (a book of the Bible) that is short, preferably one that contains one to six chapters and can be read in its entirety at one sitting. To become entirely familiar with the aromas and flavors from this treat, you should read the same book five times before you get into truly dining — studying the book as a whole.

The Menu

Scripture: Song of Solomon 2:4
"He has brought me to His Banquet Hall,
and His banner over me is love"

The menu is designed for today's modern authentic Christian to give you an overview of what has been especially selected and prepared for the Christian's dining pleasure in the pages of this book. It provides detailed instructions introducing the menu items and is a powerful tool to establish and reinforce the total concept of God's meal plan for the Christian. It deals with the responsibilities of the Christian in all areas of life.

Each menu contains spiritual recipes that were designed by the Master Chef, Jesus Christ, with a sophisticated flare. These will be served to you dish by dish so that you may taste and experience every bit of the flavor from his spices of love and sweet herbs of compassion and become knowledgeable about every ingredient in each dish as it is plated and served.

The spiritual table has been spread out so that the appetite of the most fastidious eater of the Word can be satisfied. There are traditional and popular dishes de jour ("of" or "from the day") as well as those dishes that reflect the culture in which we live. The tasty desserts include dishes such as the *vol-au-dent of fruit,* a spiritual puff pastry filled with fruits and baked to perfection. These desserts represent characters in the Bible who were perfectly fruitful in their obedience to God.

Each menu was developed to tell the Christian what soul food items are available in each meal and how much they cost. They reveal the preparation of the meal and what garnishes were used to complete it. Most important is the fact that we as gentiles will be served the message so we can become genteel.

If you choose to dine a la carte, picking just one item to dine on extensively, then your dining experience calls for certain types of advance work, and *mise en place* will help you adjust to the flow of the meal. Mise en place simply means putting everything in order before you eat your spiritual meal. Consult the menu to see what you will be dining on and then read the recipe's ingredients carefully so that you will understand all that was involved in preparing the meal. It is good to read through the entire menu to gain an understanding of exactly what will be required to complete it. Although these meals consist of many components, all of them have a good supply of nutrients for the believer.

The Royal Family's Main Secret Ingredient: Jesus Christ

The King used his own Special Main Secret Ingredient in all of the sixty-six meals (books) found in the Great Recipe Book so that you could taste and see that the Lord is good. Our Lord and Savior, the Lamb of God, is *the Royal Family Secret Main Ingredient* that was passed down from generation to generation (Genesis to Revelation). This Secret Ingredient has been listed in each meal as a "hint" to assist you in finding out how the Lamb is included. The Lamb is the foundational, high-quality stock used in each meal to create the many strong, flavorful spiritual cuisines found in God's Word.

Do not be deceived into thinking that those outside the family of God have created great cuisines by changing the recipes of the Master Chef. They have made foolish attempts to serve you imitations of spiritual meals, but their meals lack in quality, taste and nutritional value because they have excluded the most important Ingredient. These meals are useless because they can't build you up or give you eternal life. The Main Secret Ingredient of the Master Chef's meals can only be found and extracted from the flesh and blood of the Lamb.

Appetizers: Word and Term Studies

Hors d'oeuvres is a French term that means "outside the meal." In English these are usually called appetizers. Hot or cold, they are meant to stimulate your appetite. Appetizers are usually bite-sized, but they are very labor intensive to make and must be considered when entrees are prepared because they are designed to logically connect to the courses that follow. They are small portions of very flavorful foods that are meant to take just enough edge off your appetite to permit a thorough enjoyment of the entrees. In this devotional cookbook, *appetizers* are words and terms. You will need to study them in order to gain a clear understanding of the meal. In studying this portion of each lesson, you will need to use your *dinner fork* and *salad fork* (your concordance and Bible dictionary) to find out how various words are used in the context of the Bible passage. This is important because some words have different meanings based on different situations and contexts, or different Greek or Hebrew words may underlie the English being used in different Scripture passages. The most important factor is to determine the true meaning of the word or term to fully understand how it is used in that particular Scripture. Reading cross-references (other Scriptures related to the text) will give you additional insight.

Oftentimes, there are words that are repeated in Scripture. These are keywords that are important to consider in studying. Some words are significant even though they have not been repeated, but they are emphasized. But when God repeats himself, it's not because he forgot what he said to us. He is making an important point, and we need to take notice.

Word study is about finding out what is meant by the word used. Correctly interpreting the Bible will depend on having a correct understanding of the words used to convey the truth. Write down what the original word means by using your concordance and/or Bible dictionary to find out how the word is used in that particular Scripture.

When you start to taste and learn from the appetizers used in your meals, you will need to record your discoveries so you can refer back to them as you dine on the entrée. Studying the Bible by words and terms will help you gain meaningful insight into what Scripture is actually saying to

10 Recipes for Godly Living

you as opposed to what you either want it to say or think it is saying.

- Use the Word and Term Study Form (listed under Study Forms) to complete your word and term studies.

Salads: Verse to Verse Study

When you get into eating your salads (individual verses), you will need to consider every spiritual vegetable or fruit item included in the blend of incredible choices from the Master Chef, Jesus Christ. The spiritual vegetables and fruits you need to look for in the verses of Scripture are the parables, miracles, conversations between the Lord and people, prayers, and events.

If possible, pick a verse from each chapter you wish to memorize. Write that verse on an index card to carry around and review whenever possible. "Thy Word have I hid in my heart that I may not sin against thee" *(Psalm 119:11).*

The *main house salad* in each lesson has been chosen to assist you in summarizing the book you are studying. We suggest you choose a verse that speaks to you personally and put that verse to memory. This could be a verse that God wants you to apply to your life. This verse will come in handy when God gives you an opportunity to use it in a specific situation or during difficult times when you need to encourage yourself or someone else.

- Use the Verse to Verse Study Form (listed under Study Forms) to complete your verse study.

The Recipe

Ingredients: Themes

The list of ingredients used is the suggested main theme(s) for each meal, and it describes what is included in the recipe.

The Recipe of the Meal: Book Summary

The *Recipe of the Meal* is a summary of the book you are studying. The recipe was written to assist you in gaining a general understanding of the ingredients used in the meal before you begin analyzing each entrée. The recipes were written to record all of the ingredients in the meal to help you prepare for a particular entrée.

Entrée: Chapter Study

Enjoying your entrée is studying the Bible by chapters. You will concentrate on this section of each lesson in order to discover the outline for the chapter. Every chapter should have an outline, and every chapter should yield at least one great truth for you to discover. When you discover who Jesus is in the chapters, you will list that as a great truth. Chapter study, also referred to as chapter analysis, is analyzing each chapter of the book you are studying. Chapter study enables you to gain a delicious knowledge of the "recipe" as a whole.

To gain a thorough understanding of each chapter, you will need to examine each paragraph, each verse, and the particular words used. The individual portions of the meal you previously ate will assist you in this part of your study. Studying the entrées will enable you to receive knowledge of the Bible in the way it was intended and not just the way you think it should be.

- Use the Chapter Study Form (listed under Study Forms) to complete your chapter study.

Desserts: Character Study

This portion of the meal involves a delicious collection of fat-free, low-calorie ingredients: the characters in God's

Recipe Book, the Bible. However, you will also discover some desserts that are high-calorie and bad for you. Separating your character desserts will help in your knowledge of what is good and what is bad to digest when you later prepare your healthy dietary and weight loss programs.

Suggestion: There are some great desserts to choose from in the Bible that are really tasty—and good for you too! It is always good to find out if their names have meaning. The meaning of their names will further assist you in understanding why they are included in the Master Chef's recipes and can offer some clarification to the text.

These desserts are either fat-free treats you won't want to skip or full of calories that are not good for you, so you need to know what is in them so you can avoid them. The fat-free, low-calorie desserts are those characters that have good qualities we need to take notice of. The desserts that are full of calories are those characters that have sin in their lives or are disobedient to God. We want to take notice of them as well to make sure our characteristics are not matching up with those God has dealt harshly with because of their sin and disobedience.

The character study for each meal is a list of the most

important people or character descriptions used in the books you are studying. These desserts are consumed by asking yourself, who are the main people in the book? You should want to know why they are mentioned, why they are described the way they are, and what is so significant about them that God felt it was important to include them in his recipes. Consider who they are, what they do, and the consequences behind their actions, whether they are positive or negative; write these down to help you in preparing your healthy dietary and weight loss programs, which are explained later on.

When studying characters, it is good to observe their strengths, weaknesses, shortcomings, and outstanding qualities. Character study will give insight into how you can conform to the standards of God and become more Christ-like. Identify the characteristics of their lives that illustrate the truths taught in the Bible. Especially look for their outstanding characteristics. What impressed you about this character that would cause you to give notice, and what part does he or she play in the Bible? Search for positive characteristics that you can take on to enhance your character. Remember that a sweet treat at the end of a good meal can be very satisfying, especially when you start your own collection of irresistible, delicious desserts that can become your favorite treats.

The Chief Desserts (*Godhead Characters*): The Father, Son, and Holy Spirit

God is the chief character in the Scriptures. It's mainly important while dining to notice what names God the Father, God the Son, and God the Holy Spirit use to describe themselves while interacting with mankind. Look for statements that tell you about their love, compassion, holiness, justice, grace, mercy, power, patience, loving-kindness, strength, authority, hand (control), faithfulness, anger, and wrath. This will give you the knowledge of who they are in all their glory. The topping for this dessert will be the beginning of wisdom; which you will taste first, because you will have firsthand knowledge and understanding as you discover the almighty power and authority they possess. The whipped cream on top of this special dessert will be very sweet because you will taste God's loving-kindness that will provide you with the sweet treats of blessings to end every meal.

Dancing with The King

Very Special Spiritual Treat

There is one really special treat unlike all the other spiritual treats mentioned, and it is to dance with the King during the banquet feast. To dance with the King simple means to receive guidance. This is when you allow the King to guide you through his Word and keep you in his will for your life.

When you take a close look at the word *guidance,* you see G, U, I, and *dance,* which says, "God, You and I Dance." However, dancing requires one partner taking the lead while the other partner follows. Notice the order of the letters in this word. This is clearly an indication of the position of the two who dance together. God comes first. He needs to take first position in order to guide you. It's natural for the King to take the lead because he knows all the right moves to make and all the right steps to take to keep you in sync with whatever song is playing in your life. It becomes a big problem for you when you try to take the lead and get ahead of God because you're not familiar with every song that is going to play, so trying to lead could cause you to step on the King's toes, get off beat, or even miss a beat. This will throw you off balance and may even cause you to stumble and fall.

Just imagine dancing with the King when he wraps his loving arms around you while holding you close to him to keep you from moving in the wrong direction as you dance to the different melodies of life. It's such a beautiful sight to see the King dancing as the two of you partner up to become one in Christ. The melody is so sweet and feels so good when we are in harmony with the King. In this intimate relationship with the King, we will find that he loves to dance with us, especially if we let him take the lead. When I allow the King to guide me, the rhythm is so smooth and the moves are just so right that I can't help but say, "God, You and I dance divinely."

If you find yourself stepping on the King's toes every now and then, or maybe falling down because your rhythm is off and you are out of step with the King, it's because you have been taking the lead. You probably need to ask the King to give you some dancing lessons—he's a great dance instructor and is willing to pick you up off the dance floor of life to take the lead again. He will guide you in the right direction where the melody of the song is sweet and get you back in step with him to make all the right moves.

GUIDANCE: *Deuteronomy 3 2 : 1 2 , Psalm 23:2, Psalm 48:14, and John 16:13*

Your Spiritual Fitness Program

The *Weight Loss Program* is a life-changing application process that is based on the list you have personally developed around the characters in the Bible. You will plan to lose the sins that were committed by the characters in the Bible, but also the contaminated foods in your spiritual body, the trans- fats and bitter herbs (sins) that bring spiritual food-borne illnesses that will give you food poisoning and destroy the spiritual body. Spiritual food-borne illnesses are caused by digesting *perverted*, *adulterated*, and *fornicated* foods that are contaminated with spiritual viruses, parasites, and bacteria that are unfit for human consumption. The spiritual viruses, parasites, and bacteria are those unseen "rulers, authorities, powers of this dark world and the spiritual forces of evil in the heavenly realms" (Ephesians 6:12) that are controlled by Satan and used to attack the weak parts of your spiritual immune system. These free radicals are the unstable and highly reactive schemes Satan uses to tempt you with that can damage the spiritual body because they accelerate the progression of spiritual cancer cells and also cause cardiovascular diseases that affect your heart.

Trans-fats are far more lethal than we realize because they have the ability to reduce the level of good in us. You can be spiritually overweight because of a high fat (sin) intake, which is associated with and contributes to such conditions as spiritual heart disease and spiritual death. We are faced with different challenges in life, and to move in the right direction, we need to eliminate the trans-fats and bitter herbs from our diets and then consider an alternative menu that contains zero grams of fat and makes everything work out for our good and God's glory. Based on what you are going to learn from your meals, you will need to eliminate these sinful foods from your system in order to have a healthy heart and spiritual body fit for you to continue in building your relationship with the King.

The *Healthy Dietary Program* contains spiritual proteins that the Master Chef, Jesus Christ, placed in spiritual foods used in his Great Recipe Book. These are major components of the Word, with nutritional value that supplies energy and helps you maintain a healthy heart and spiritual body. In order to commit to making a conscious effort to change by transforming your mind, you need to list those life-changing behaviors, attitudes, habits, personalities, characteristics, and practices that you should indulge in to improve the quality of your life for God and for those around you whom you love.

When considering your health and what foods are good to eat to be completely successful, you will find that every good diet always includes a healthy exercise program to keep you in shape. The more you exercise, the better you will feel and the less likely you will be to become weak and sickly. Exercising, in this case, simply means personally applying God's Word.

The *Exercise Program* is the daily activity used to enable you to build up the muscles in your spiritual body to give you the strength needed to perform your spiritual weight-lifting responsibilities as a believer. No plan for a healthy life would be complete without this exercise program. In order to perfect the "temple," a true believer needs to perform the following exercises to keep every part of the spiritual body functioning to its fullest potential. To assist you in keeping active and your spiritual body working properly so you can flex those muscles, you must:

Exercise your *love* for the King and for one another.
God commands us to love him with all of our heart, soul, and

might *(Deuteronomy 6:5 and Matthew 22:37)*. Since one of his attributes is love, he requires that we be full of love for him and for one another. In order to exercise our love for God, we must learn what is required to love him the way he expects to be loved.

God commands us to love one another as he has loved us. He has placed the Holy Spirit within us so that we can build one another up in the royal family of God, and we should never tear one another down in the royal court (the church).

Exercise your *faith* in the King and not in man.

God tells us in his word that without faith, it is impossible to please him *(Hebrews 11:6)*. He wants us to be totally dependent on him and no one else.

Exercise your *obedience* to the King so that you will know his will for your life.

Our loyalty to God should be reflected in our obedience, which should be one of our most outstanding characteristics as princes or princesses in Christ Jesus *(1 Samuel 15:22: "Obedience is better than sacrifice")*. As Christ humbled himself, becoming obedient to his Father's will, we too must humble ourselves in order to become obedient to God, seeking not our own will in the process but the will of our heavenly Father. You can trust that the will of God will never take you where his grace will not protect you.

Exercise your *forgiveness* toward one another.

God commands us to forgive one another from the heart *(Matthew 18:35)*, as he has forgive us from his heart. Forgiveness implies a release or setting a person free. It is a dismissal or a suspension of a just penalty or guilt, so real forgiveness does not set up conditions that must be met before you can forgive someone, especially in the royal court (the church).

Exercise your *prayers* to communicate with the King on a daily basis.

Prayer is simply conversing directly with or addressing God. It is important to pray about everything, regardless of how big or small the need. You want to become totally dependent on God to direct and guide you in every situation and circumstance. He wants to hear from you on a regular basis about everything that concerns you.

Exercise your *spiritual gifts* to build up the kingdom of the King.

To exercising your spiritual gifts is to exercise your skills and abilities in the church. Using your gifts is also a form of worship to God. Romans 12:1 tells us, *"Present your bodies a living sacrifice, holy, acceptable unto God, which is your reasonable service."*

Compliments to the Master Chef: New Songs of Praise
The compliments to the Master Chef included after each spiritual meal are those praises of thanksgiving we express when we discover the amazing knowledge that is revealed to us during our reading and studying of God's Word. These compliments should be written down, memorized, and repeated during the day.

Proper Royal Fine Dining Etiquette

Proper dining etiquette is one aspect of the decorum that is expected to govern your behavior within the King's court. Proper royal etiquette reflects various formulas of conduct which the Master Chef invested his time and energy in developing. They fundamentally prescribe and restrict the ways in which you interact with the King because you show your proper respect for him by conforming to the etiquette norms.

As a prince or princess, you are adorned with God's royal attire, the full armor of God found in Ephesians 6:13–17, and you have been given a spiritual signet ring to wear in order as an eternal sign of "Holiness to the Lord." This ring is to signify to the world that there is no end to your holiness before the Lord and man.

Your royal attire is the armor to be worn as you go about your day. It is your protection against evil and the Evil One. First, the Belt of Truth is buckled around your waist. The Belt of Truth is crucial, because a child of the King who is dishonest cannot hope to withstand any weapon aimed at him or her by Satan, the father of lies. The truth here is synonymous with integrity and should be seen as a life of practicing honesty and truthfulness. It is also the truth that protects who we are in Christ Jesus.

Another piece of our royal attire is the Breastplate of Righteousness, full of faith and love. In Roman times, the breastplate went completely around the body, which also protected the warrior's back. Our faith and love for Christ Jesus will fully protect us from any surprise attacks coming from any direction. The righteousness seen here is the righteous character and deeds of the believer. The breastplate is also used to seek judgment. As difficult situations arise in our life, we are to respond with the right spirit by seeking decisions from the Lord regarding any issue requiring divine discernment. This piece of attire is placed over your heart as a reminder of your responsibility before the King. In the Old Testament, the priest's breastplate held two mysterious stones called the Thummim and the Urim. The Hebrew translation of these two words means *Perfections and Lights.* Together, their names could be interpreted to mean "perfect knowledge." Perfect knowledge only comes from God, who will place the proper decisions in our hearts when we seek his counsel.

Then we have our feet shod (or shoed) with the readiness that comes from the gospel of peace as we walk the streets of this world. The shoes represent the preparation of the gospel of peace, which means that the gospel is the firm foundation on which we as believers are to stand and which we are to be ready to defend as well as spreading the gospel. These sandals also keep us standing firmly planted in the peaceful will of God.

In addition to this, you should always have on the Shield of Faith, which is used to extinguish all of the flaming arrows thrown at you by your jealous, unseen spiritual enemy and adversary, Satan. He and his army of demons will viciously attack, seeking to kill, steal, and destroy you if you are not properly dressed. This shield is no small piece of the armor, because it covers the entire royal attire and represents God's protection against all attacks from the Wicked One (Psalm 28:7: "The Lord is my strength and my shield; my heart trusts in Him, and I am helped").

As a royal prince or princess, you are given a royal crown to wear with your royal attire. In the Old Testament crowns were made with an overlay of pure gold, but the crown that rests on your forehead is the Helmet of Salvation, which should be adorned with jewels of wisdom and which carries a spiritual engraving that says "Holiness to the Lord" as you come into a right relationship with the King. The Helmet of Salvation will protect our heads when we put on the mind of Christ, which gives us wisdom and discernment.

To complete your royal attire, you must carry the Sword of the Spirit with you at all times, which is the Word of God. The Sword of the Spirit is the only offensive weapon needed, ready to be spoken in specific situations and considered in all circumstances. We can combat all of Satan's lies when we use the truth from Scripture to defend ourselves and defeat our spiritual enemy.

We should never be seen or found without our complete royal attire on because it will protect us from the demonic forces that work through those Satan uses to attack us. This royal attire is considered our holy garments, and they are made holy by our consecration to God's service. They represent the concept of our imputed righteousness before the Lord *(Zechariah 3:1-5)*. The royal attire symbolizes our character and behavior, because the Scripture describes our behavior as the clothes we wear. In 1 Peter 5:5, Peter tells us to be "clothed with humility." The attire Jesus wore was made of perfection because it was a robe that was seamless. Isaiah 61:10 says, "I will rejoice greatly in the Lord . . . for He has clothed me with garments of salvation; He has wrapped me with a robe of righteousness." The Lord has provided us with this special attire to meet all of the daily challenges we will face each day we live.

In the Old Testament, God instructed the Israelites to tie tassels on the end of their robes as a reminder to never forget what God had done for them. We too are expected not to forsake our King who has blessed and kept us. We are also expected to remember our royal position and what the King and Master Chef has done for us, because in remembering we will be less likely to stray away from our royal responsibilities and sin against him by having a desire to turn back to a previous state of being without God.

An abundance of blessings has been given to us. It is a privilege to have been cleaned up, given royal attire to wear, and brought near to the King. We were put in his palace to have total access to the King at all times and to feast on his banquet of spiritual food whenever we desire it, never to experience hunger or thirst again in life because Jesus said in John 6:35, "I am the Bread of Life; he who comes to Me will not hunger, and he who believes in Me will never thirst." You have complete access to eat the *True Food* and drink the *True Drink,* which are the flesh and blood of Jesus Christ, so that he can abide in you and you in him *(John 6:55).*

Unfortunately, some of us have violated our royal position by not learning the proper etiquette required of a child of God. Violations of proper etiquette can cause public disgrace and private hurt for those who misrepresent the kingdom, and they create misunderstanding among the royal court, the church. Public disgrace comes from not eating enough spiritual food from the King's table and then being caught off guard when we are approached by those outside the holy family who question us about our King, our royal position as a prince or princess, and our beliefs in Jesus Christ. Private hurt can be caused when we haven't become skillful in using the Sword of Spirit and we can't be sanctified to the Lord God in our hearts and ready always to give an answer to every man who asks us a reason of the hope that is in us with meekness and fear *(1 Peter 3:15).*

Of course, we all know that it is not proper etiquette to eat a meal without the proper utensils so we can scoop up every morsel of food without wasting it on our royal attire. A list of fine dining utensils (resource tools) has been included to assist you to feast on your spiritual meals.

While sitting at the spiritual dinner table, you will need to use:

- **A Sharp Knife: Study Bible.** Hebrews 4:12 tells us that God's Word is like a two-edged sword. The Bible is an important tool to learn how to handle. Consistent use of this fine silverware will assist you in gaining the skillful cutting techniques required to properly slice up the meat of the Word without seriously cutting yourself on the sharpness of the knife by misquoting Scripture or taking it out of its context. A good study Bible is the first and foremost utensil to use when feasting on spiritual foods in God's Word.

- **A Dinner Fork: Concordance.** The dinner fork is used for picking out selected portions of food to chew on (meditate) and digest (understand) to assist in the nourishment of your soul. It is important in consuming your appetizers—words and terms—as well.

- **A Salad Fork: Bible Dictionary or Bible Encyclopedia.** These two utensils are extremely valuable for word study because they help distinguish those salad mixtures of subjects, words, places, and doctrines that need to be understood fully in context. Some salad forks include illustrations, genealogical tables, maps, and other information that will bring freshness to the spiritual vegetables and fruits of the text.

- **A Soup Spoon: Commentary.** The soup spoon is used for stirring and mixing spiritual ingredients to smooth out any lumps of misunderstanding when a passage of Scripture does not seem clear to you.

- **A Dessert Fork: Bible Handbook.** The dessert fork is a helpful piece of silverware used to pick up sweet and irresistible information about every book in the Bible. The dessert fork helps to serve up delicious and fascinating treats about archeological findings and the four hundred years of silence between the Old and New Testaments.

These utensils can be found on the following websites:

- www.studylight.org
- www.blueletterbible.org
- www.bible.org

These fine dining utensils can help to alleviate some of the problems the King's children may experience when exercising their responsibilities as royalty as they eat the Word of God and apply what they are learning.

Spiritual Fundamental Eating Concepts and Procedures

The Royal Family Banquet Table Setting

Food *handlers of God's Word* must learn to use the proper methods and utensils in their dining experience. As you go through the lessons in this book, you will be instructed to read a selected book of the Bible at one sitting and repeat your reading of the same book five times. This is considered devotional reading, or what I consider a part of your Royal Candlelight moments, where you are just sitting before the Lord to read his Word. Again, this can be done early in the morning before you start your day. Rising early in the morning to meet Jesus is what Jesus did when he rose up to meet with God to commune with him.

To help yourself commit to this daily routine, decide to eat a spiritual meal before you eat a physical one — in other words, unless you have to for health reasons, make a commitment not to eat breakfast until you have read God's Word. Just in case you are not a breakfast eater, try not to eat *any* physical food until you have eaten at least a spiritual breakfast bar or snack (a chapter or two in the Bible every day and at least five chapters on Sunday). This means you may have to get up fifteen or twenty minutes earlier to feed your spiritual body before going about your busy day.

The following procedures will help you get the most of out of your daily dining in the Word of God.

1. **Before you start eating,** *season your food with prayer.*

   Prayer is one of the most important skills to develop. Seasoning enhances the natural flavor of food without significantly changing its flavor. Saying grace (or giving thanks to God) before every meal is an appropriate practice. Before you began any Bible study, you should pray for God to enhance your taste for him so you will be able to "taste and see that the Lord is good." *(Psalm 34:8)*

   Pray to be forgiven, because you don't want to come to the royal dinner table with dirty hands. Pray to be cleansed of all unrighteousness — it's like freshening up or bathing before you eat dinner. You will have the privilege of dining with the King as the Royal Candlelight shines brightly in the middle of the royal dinner table. You should delight in being in the presence of God to make your fellowship time meaningful and joyful, especially while studying his Word. It's a great joy to be in the presence of God, coming together with him as one in love.

While you are at the dinner table, try to meditate, which is prayerful thinking and concentration on the meal, and ask the Master Chef to show you how to apply these nutritious meals for your good to make you a pleasing sight to him and to give him glory.

2. **Take your personally prescribed spiritual vitamins and supplements of praise and worship.**

Your personal prescription of vitamins and supplements of praise and worship are important to enhance the nutritional quality of your food, and they will help to regulate your body functions. So spend a moment telling the King how much you appreciate these specially prepared meals, blended just for you with skillfully selected flavors of exquisite spices of love and sweet herbs of compassion. It will be a pleasingly sweet aroma if you take time to bless the Lord with praise and worship. You will also become familiar with each spice's aroma, its flavor, and the effect that it has on the food you are about to eat.

3. **Don't forget to ask the King for the Aged Royal Wine that goes with every meal to help you digest your food. We suggest you drink a *full* glass of the Holy Spirit, which complements every meal.** Ephesians 5:18 tells us, "Do not get drunk with wine, for that is dissipation, but be filled with the Spirit." The Holy Spirit is the One who teaches us everything we need to know about the Word of God. This drink releases the exquisite flavors of joy, peace, patience, kindness, goodness, faithfulness, gentleness, and self-control, which sweeten the taste of the knowledge of Christ Jesus. There are no added preservatives or passion fruits of desire mixed in this drink (Galatians 5:22).

The Holy Spirit is not only the special fruit drink you will need to go with every meal, but it comes with a seal of approval directly from the Master Chef, Jesus Christ, that guarantees your safety against digesting any food-borne illnesses (Ephesians 1:14: "who is a deposit guaranteeing our inheritance until the redemption of those who are God's possession — to the praise of His glory.")

4. **When dining by Royal Candlelight at the royal dinner table, when possible, read the book you have selected at one sitting** so you don't leave anything on your plate. This will help you grasp a general knowledge about what you will be studying, and again, this can be done during your devotional moments with God. In instances when the books of the Bible are too long to read at one sitting, decide on what chapters you are going to read each day until you've read the entire book.

5. **Repeat the reading of the same book five times** to familiarize yourself with the savory flavors you will taste before you begin to digest your food. Reading the book repeatedly enables you to feel the flow of the book you are about to study. Try reading Scripture in different translations as well. This will give you additional insights as you view each translator's rendering of the original writing. Take notes on the interesting discoveries from reading repeatedly and the

differences in each translation.

6. **While dining by Royal Candlelight at the royal dinner table, write down what is revealed to you during your conversation with the King as he tells you how the Master Chef, Jesus Christ, has prepared the food that is before you.** *Spend time chewing your food (meditating) so you can enjoy every bite.* This is a good time to get to know God and develop an intimate relationship by asking him questions about the irresistible recipes you are feasting on. Meditating is taking the necessary time to think and process what you have read. Allowing the truth to sink in helps prepare you to live out what you have learned. It also gives you an opportunity to readjust every area of your life where necessary.

Joshua 1:8 and Psalm 1:1-2 both tell us to meditate on the Word of God day and night. Meditation is a time when you can ask yourself if there is some part of your life where the truth is needed to better your life.

7. **Pick *verse salads* that you can put to memory to go along with the chapter *entrées* you're eating.** Learn what spiritual vegetables and fruits make up the salads, and pick out the Main House Salad for each entrée (the key verse of the chapter). Study and take note of all the ingredients in each salad you choose. Is their texture raw so that you have to spend some time chewing (meditating) on them to gain an understanding, or were they cooked for tenderness so they are quicker and easier to swallow (understand)? When you have gained more experience with your salads, you will know what ingredients contribute to the flavor and how they function in our spiritual bodies after we consume them.

Chapter 6

10 Meal Lessons

Scripture: Luke 14: 16-17
"But He said to him, A certain man was giving a big
dinner, and he invited many; and at the dinner hour he
sent his slave to say to those who had been invited, Come;
for everything is ready now."

10 Spiritual Meal Lessons

The *following* *ten meal lessons* reflect how the Secret Main Ingredient, the Lamb, was used in each meal to provide the nutritional value needed for each prince and princess to digest and gain spiritual strength. The Lamb supplies the blood stream with all the spiritual strength and nutrients required for every child of God to become spiritually strong and healthy.

New Testament Meals

Meals	The Royal Family Secret Ingredient
Matthew	Jesus is Our Savior, the Christ
Mark	Jesus is The Perfect Servant
Luke	Jesus is The Son of Man
John	Jesus is The Son of God
Acts	Jesus is The Prince of Life
Romans	Jesus is Our Righteousness
1 Corinthians	Jesus is Our Gift
2 Corinthians	Jesus is Our Justification
Hebrews	Jesus is My Intercessor
Revelation	Jesus is Alpha and Omega

Get ready to discover the Light that is shining from the center of the King's big banquet table on each spiritual meal you will dine on. It will illuminate the importance of the characteristics and attributes of Jesus Christ and the importance of each position he holds in relationship to you as his child while you feast on his delicious spiritual meals.

Chapter 7

"YOUR ROYAL DINNER IS SERVED"
from
10 RECIPES FOR GODLY LIVING

PRINCE and PRINCESS

Be prepared to dine sufficiently with The King

Sit down and take you rightful place at the King's Royal Banquet Table, where the *Royal Candlelight* has been placed in the very center of the King's Table for you to enjoy the Light and the Meal.

§

Say grace, dig in, and taste and see just how great the ***LAMB*** taste to all of you who feast abundantly on the word of God.

Bon Appétit!
A French Term Meaning – I Wish You A Hearty Appetite!

MATTHEW

Sous Chef: Matthews   ***Date Meal Prepared***: *Between AD 55–65*

Menu

The Royal Family Secret Ingredient:
Jesus Is Our Savior, the Christ

Your meal for today consists of understanding our salvation from the deity of Christ and his earthly mission to save us. We learn the importance of putting our faith in the One and Only True and Living God because our salvation comes through the *birth, life, death, and resurrection* of Jesus Christ, the Messiah. The Eternal King proves this by fulfilling the Old Testament prophecies.

1. Season your food with prayer and take your spiritual vitamins and supplements of praise and worship before you start eating your meal.

2. If necessary, review the Spiritual Fundamental Eating Concepts and Procedures for further instruction.

3. Pick a few *salads* that you can put to memory to go along with some of the *entrées* you're going to dine on. Then, "pack a lunch for tomorrow" by writing them

down on an index card and putting the card in an index box to carry your favorite spiritual salads with you. Dine on them during your lunch break—feed both your physical and spiritual sides at the same time. Study and take note of all the ingredients in each salad you choose. (Job 23:12: "I have treasured the words of His mouth more than my necessary food.")

4. The Main House Salad (key verse) is listed under the salad menu below.

Appetizers

Needed: *Sharp Knife, Dinner Fork, and Salad Forks*

To give you a better understanding from the chapters, indulge in an appetizer! Determine the true meaning of the following words and/or terms by using your concordance and Bible dictionary to fully understand how they are used after you have read the chapter. Use your Word and Term Study Form to record your dining discoveries:

1. Repent
2. Blessed
3. Anxious
4. False Prophets
5. Fruit (*Good and Bad*)

6. Disciples
7. Prayer and Fasting
8. Salvation
9. Lawlessness
10. Prudent
11. Talent
12. Kingdom of Heaven (*Kingdom of God*)

Salad

Needed: *Sharp Knife, Dinner Fork and Soup Spoon*

Suggested Main House Salad: Matthew 16:16: "And Simon Peter answered and said, Thou art the *Christ*, the Son of the *living God.*"

Use your Verse to Verse Study Form to record your choice salads. What spiritual salad(s) did you choose to pack for your lunch tomorrow?

Recipe for MATTHEW
Book Summary

Ingredients (Themes): Jesus the Messiah; the Kingdom of God; Love; Salvation; Answered Prayers; God's Presence; Excellence.

The Gospel According to Matthew focuses on the birth, life, death, and resurrection of Jesus Christ, the Messiah. Matthew proclaims God's redemption plan, which was fulfilled through Jesus. We see the introduction, the development, and the completion of Jesus's ministry here on earth, which clearly shows that Jesus is Christ (Matthew 1:16).

Even though the message of the kingdom was only for the Jews during Christ's lifetime here on earth, Jesus commissioned his disciples to go to "all nations" to preach the gospel, which includes the Gentiles, because they along with the Jews are co-heirs of the kingdom of God.

Entrées

Needed: *Sharp Knife and Dinner Fork*

Read and examine each chapter of this book. Use your Chapter Study Form to complete this portion of the menu. (Don't forget the spiritual appetizers you've chosen to go with some of your entrees).

- **Chapter 1** – The Genealogy of Jesus Christ
- **Chapter 2** – The Visit of the Wise Men
- **Chapter 3** – The Baptism of Jesus
- **Chapter 4** – Forty Days of the Temptation of Jesus
- **Chapter 5** – The Sermon on the Mount
- **Chapter 6** – Charity and Prayer

- **Chapter 7** – Judging Others
- **Chapter 8** – Jesus Cleanses a Leper
- **Chapter 9** – Jesus Heals a Paralytic
- **Chapter 10** – Instructions for the Twelve Disciples
- **Chapter 11** – Tribute to John the Baptist
- **Chapter 12** – Lord of the Sabbath
- **Chapter 13** – The Parables of Jesus
- **Chapter 14** – John the Baptist Beheaded
- **Chapter 15** – Tradition and Commandment
- **Chapter 16** – The Pharisees Test Jesus
- **Chapter 17** – The Transfiguration of Jesus
- **Chapter 18** – Who Is the Greatest in the Kingdom
- **Chapter 19** – Questions about Divorce
- **Chapter 20** – Laborers in the Vineyard
- **Chapter 21** – The Triumphal Entry
- **Chapter 22** – Marriage Feast Parable
- **Chapter 23** – The Woes of the Scribes and the Pharisees
- **Chapter 24** – Signs of Christ's Return
- **Chapter 25** – The Parable of the Ten Virgins
- **Chapter 26** – The Plot to Kill Jesus
- **Chapter 27** – Judas Officially Condemned
- **Chapter 28** – Jesus Is Risen

Desserts

Needed: *Sharp Knife, Soup Spoon, and Salad Fork*

List the qualities of each character, both positive and negative. Use the Character Study Form to record your taste of what is good or bad about each dessert to see if they were bitter or sweet. (Don't forget to include what you've learn from these desserts in your spiritual weight loss and healthy dietary programs.)

- Jesus *(The Messiah)*
- Jesus *(Savior and King)*
- Matthew *(Levi)*
- Heavenly Father
- Herod the King
- John the Baptist
- Pharisees
- King of the Jews
- Mary Magdalene
- Judas

Menu Lessons (Questions)

Since you have dined sufficiently on this meal, explain what you digested by answering the following questions:

1. How did Matthew prove that Jesus is the Messiah?
2. How does the Gospel of Matthew link the Old and the New Testaments?
3. What are the five major discourses of Christ in the book of Matthew?

Describe in your own words the savory flavors or sweet aromas that come from this meal.

- Describe your gourmet fine dining experience after you have learned that *Jesus is Our Savior, the Christ.*

Here are some "After-Dinner Mints and Sweet Treats" (Promises and Blessings) for you to enjoy.
"Thank You for Dining with Us"

- *Our heavenly Father will forgive us*
- *We are granted the knowledge of the mysteries of the kingdom of heaven*
- *With God all things are possible*
- *Jesus's life is a ransom for many*

See what other promises and blessings you find in the book of Matthew that are sweet to you after you have dined sufficiently. Use your Daily Bread Spiritual Journal to record the promises and blessings you discover.

Compliments to the Master Chef

Here are just a few compliments you can consider as you begin to look for every opportunity in the book of Matthew to praise God when you respond to this delicious meal. Sing a new song of praise that you have never sung before now.

- *Praise God for being with us (Matthew 1:23)*
- *Praise God for the Spirit who speaks to us (Matthew 10:20)*
- *Praise God for his yoke is easy and his burden is light (Matthew 11:30)*
- *Praise God for the Son of the Living God (Matthew 16:16)*
- *Praise God for the greatness of a servant (Matthew 20:26)*

MARK

Sous Chef: Mark   ***Date Meal Prepared:*** *Between AD 55–60*

Menu

The Royal Family Secret Ingredient:
Jesus is The Perfect Servant

Your meal for today consists of learning how we should serve the needs of others as we make life sacrifices for those who are less fortunate than ourselves. You will digest (*understand*) the demonstration of a Perfect Servant in Jesus Christ, who served as a perfect example of how we ourselves are to perfectly serve others.

1. Season your food with prayer and take your spiritual vitamins and supplements of praise and worship before you start eating your meal.

2. If necessary, review the Spiritual Fundamental Eating Concepts and Procedures for further instruction.

3. Pick a few *salads* that you can put to memory to go along with some of the *entrées* you're going to dine on. Then, "pack a lunch for tomorrow" by writing them down on an index card and putting the card in an index box to carry your favorite spiritual salads with you.

Dine on them during your lunch break—feed both your physical and spiritual sides at the same time. Study and take note of all the ingredients in each salad you choose.

4. The Main House Salad (key verse) is listed under the salad menu below.

Appetizers

Needed: *Sharp Knife, Dinner Fork, and Salad Forks*

- Servant
- Beloved Son
- Ransom
- Fishers of Men
- Demons

Salad

Needed: *Sharp Knife, Dinner Fork, and Soup Spoon*

Suggested Main House Salad: Mark 10:45: "For even the Son of Man did not come *to be served,* but *to serve,* and to *give His life a ransom* for many."

Recipe for MARK
Book Summary

Ingredients (Themes): *Jesus the Servant; Jesus as Ransom; Discipleship; Suffering and Death.*

The Gospel According to Mark focuses on Jesus's entire ministry in Galilee as Jesus accomplished his primary mission of dying for our sins. Mark shows Jesus as "the Servant" and "the Ransom" when Jesus predicts his own crucifixion. He presents the person and work of Jesus Christ.

Entrées

Needed: *Sharp Knife and Dinner Fork*

- **Chapter 1 –** The Preaching of John the Baptist
- **Chapter 2 –** A Paralytic Healed
- **Chapter 3 –** Jesus Heals on the Sabbath
- **Chapter 4 –** The Sower and the Soils Parable
- **Chapter 5 –** The Gerasene Demoniac
- **Chapter 6 –** Jesus Teaches at Nazareth
- **Chapter 7 –** Defiling the Tradition of the Pharisees
- **Chapter 8 –** Jesus Feeds Four Thousand
- **Chapter 9 –** The Transfiguration of Jesus
- **Chapter 10 –** Jesus Teaches about Divorce
- **Chapter 11 –** The Triumphal Entry
- **Chapter 12 –** The Vineyard Parable
- **Chapter 13 –** The Return of Christ
- **Chapter 14 –** The Plot to Kill Jesus
- **Chapter 15 –** The Crucifixion
- **Chapter 16 –** The Resurrection

Desserts
Needed: *Sharp Knife, Soup Spoon, and Salad Fork*

- Jesus (*Son of God*)
- Mark
- Simon
- Andrew

Menu Lessons (Questions)

Since you have dined sufficiently on this meal, explain what you digested by answering the following questions:

1. How does Mark present the person and work of Jesus Christ to the Gentiles?
2. List some of the miracles found in Mark.
3. How did the Roman culture contribute to the New Testament?

Describe in your own words the savory flavors or sweet aromas that come from this meal.

- Describe your gourmet fine dining experience after you have learned that *Jesus is The Perfect Servant.*

Here are some "After-Dinner Mints and Sweet Treats"
(Promises and Blessings) for you to enjoy.
"Thank You for Dining with Us"

- *All things are possible with God*
- *God grants us those things we pray for and believe*
- *Jesus heals*

- *Healing is for all*
- *Seeds falling on good soil grow up and increase to produce a multitude of good fruit*
- *God has blessed us with ears to hear*

Compliments to the Master Chef

- *Praise God for the great things he has done for us (Mark 5:19a)*
- *Praise God for the mercy he has on us (Mark 5:19b)*
- *Praise God for his authority over unclean spirits (Mark 6:7)*
- *Praise God for forgiveness of transgressions (Mark 11:25)*
- *Praise God for the Risen Savior (Mark 16:6)*

LUKE

Sous Chef: Luke   *Date Meal Prepared:* About AD 60

Menu

The Royal Family Secret Ingredient:
Jesus is The Son of Man

Your meal for today consists of coming into the knowledge of our long-awaited Messiah and the Savior of all mankind. We find that the Son of Man places special emphasis on his loving-kindness for the poor, the weak, the oppressed, the women, the outcasts, and all those who are suffering in various ways.

1. Season your food with prayer and take your spiritual vitamins and supplements of praise and worship before you start eating your meal.

2. If necessary, review the Spiritual Fundamental Eating Concepts and Procedures for further instruction.

3. Pick a few *salads* you can put to memory to go along with some of the *entrées* you're going to dine on. Then, "pack a lunch for tomorrow" by writing them down on an index card and putting the card in an index box to carry your favorite spiritual salads with you. Dine on

them during your lunch break—feed both your physical and spiritual sides at the same time. Study and take note of all the ingredients in each salad you choose.

4. The Main House Salad (key verse) is listed under the salad menu below.

Appetizers
Needed: *Sharp Knife, Dinner Fork, and Salad Fork*

- Holy Offspring
- Full of the Holy Spirit
- Parables
- The Beatitudes
- Hades
- Lost
- Mammon

Salad
Needed: *Sharp Knife, Dinner Fork, and Soup Spoon*
Suggested Main House Salad: Luke 19:10: "For the Son of Man has come to *seek* and to *save* that which is lost."

Recipe for LUKE
Book Summary

Ingredients (Themes): *The Son of Man; Humanity; Loving-Kindness; Forgiveness.*

The Gospel According to Luke focuses on Jesus as the perfect human as he lived and ministered here on earth. We will see how he died and then rose again to new life as Savior for all sinners. His death was a ransom to provide us with a New Covenant. We will also see the Holy Spirit being very active, from the conception of Jesus and throughout his powerful ministry. Jesus promised his followers the same powerful gift because we are sinners in need of a Savior.

Luke was a Gentile writing to a Gentile audience to present Jesus as Savior and to emphasize that the gospel is for the whole world, not just for the Jews.

Entrées

Needed: *Sharp Knife and Dinner Fork*

- **Chapter 1 –** The Introduction
- **Chapter 2 –** Jesus's Birth
- **Chapter 3 –** John the Baptist
- **Chapter 4 –** The Temptation of Jesus
- **Chapter 5 –** The Call of the First Disciples
- **Chapter 6 –** Jesus Is the Lord of the Sabbath
- **Chapter 7 –** Jesus Heals
- **Chapter 8 –** Ministering Women
- **Chapter 9 –** The Twelve Disciples Sent Forth
- **Chapter 10 –** The Seventy Sent Out
- **Chapter 11 –** Instructions on Prayer

- **Chapter 12** – The Caring and Knowledge of God
- **Chapter 13** – The Lessons in Parables
- **Chapter 14** – The Teaching of Jesus
- **Chapter 15** – The Lost
- **Chapter 16** – The Unrighteous
- **Chapter 17** – Instructions
- **Chapter 18** – The Power of Faith
- **Chapter 19** – Jesus's Last Week
- **Chapter 20** – Jesus's Authority Questioned
- **Chapter 21** – Things To Come
- **Chapter 22** – Jesus's Agony
- **Chapter 23** – The Crucifixion
- **Chapter 24** – The Ascension

Desserts

Needed: *Sharp Knife, Soup Spoon, and Salad Fork*

- Jesus (*Son of Man*)
- Luke
- Zacharias
- Gabriel (*the Angel*)
- Elizabeth
- Theophilus

Menu Lessons (Questions)

Since you have dined sufficiently on this meal, explain what you digested by answering the following questions:

1. How was Jesus presented as the Perfect Man?
2. Since you cannot serve two masters, which master have you chosen to love, serve, and hold to, and which one do you hate and despise (refer to chapter 16:13)? What is the reason for your decision?

3. What is a parable?

Describe in your own words the savory flavors or sweet aromas that come from this meal.

- Describe your gourmet fine dining experience after you have learned that *Jesus is The Son of Man.*

Here are some "After-Dinner Mints and Sweet Treats" (Promises and Blessings) for you to enjoy.
"Thank You for Dining with Us"

- *Blessed are those who hear the Word of God and observe it*
- *The Lord Jesus gives us all something to eat*
- *Nothing is impossible for God*
- *We can serve the Lord without fear*
- *The Lord is willing to make us clean*
- *We can go in peace because of faith in Christ who has saved us*
- *God's mercy is upon generation after generation*
- *We are delivered from the hand of our enemies*

Compliments to the Master Chef

- *Praise God for blessing those who believe him when he speaks (Luke 1:45)*
- *Praise God for the birth of Christ the Lord (Luke 2:11)*
- *Praise God that the Son of Man has the authority on earth to forgive us (Luke 5:24)*
- *Praise God for the Lord is the greatest among us (Luke 22:27)*

JOHN

Sous Chef: John   *Date Meal Prepared: About AD 90*

Menu

The Royal Family Secret Ingredient:
Jesus is The Son of God

Your meal for today consists of receiving everlasting life through the only begotten Son of God. The account of Jesus's life was revealed so that we would believe in the Son and not perish, but experience the gift of eternal life.

1. Season your food with prayer and take your spiritual vitamins and supplements of praise and worship before you start eating your meal.

2. If necessary, review the Spiritual Fundamental Eating Concepts and Procedures for further instruction.

3. Pick a few *salads* that you can put to memory to go along with some of the *entrées* you're going to dine on. Then, "pack a lunch for tomorrow" by writing them down on an index card and putting the card in an index box to carry your favorite spiritual salads with you. Dine on them during your lunch break—feed both your physical and spiritual sides at the same time. Study and

take note of all the ingredients in each salad you choose.

4. The Main House Salad (key verse) is listed under the salad menu below.

Appetizers
Needed: *Sharp Knife, Dinner Fork, and Salad Fork*

- In the Beginning
- The Only Begotten
- Children of God
- Disciples
- Witness
- Eternal Life

Salad
Needed: *Sharp Knife, Dinner Fork, and Soup Spoon*
Suggested Main House Salad: John 3:16: "For God so *loved the world*, that He gave His *Only Begotten Son*, that whoever *believes* in Him should not *perish*, but have *eternal life*."

Recipe for JOHN
Book Summary

Ingredients (Themes): *Jesus Is Lord; The Only Begotten Son; The Word; Christ's Return; The Holy Spirit; Blessings of Joy and Peace; Everlasting Life.*

The Gospel According to John focuses on the Son of God appearing in human form to share the life of mankind. John shows us the lordship and glory that Jesus had with the Father before the world was spoken into existence. God wanted to express himself to mankind through "The Word," Jesus Christ. The sovereignty and love of God were expressed by sending his only begotten Son to reveal himself and his plan to offer us everlasting life.

Entrées
Needed: *Sharp Knife and Dinner Fork*

- **Chapter 1** – The Deity of Jesus Christ
- **Chapter 2** – Miracles at Cana
- **Chapter 3** – The New Birth
- **Chapter 4** – The Woman in Samaria and the Nobleman's Son
- **Chapter 5** – Healings on the Sabbath
- **Chapter 6** – The Feeding of Five Thousand
- **Chapter 7** – Jesus Teaches at the Feast
- **Chapter 8** – The Adulterous Woman
- **Chapter 9** – Jesus Heals a Man Born Blind
- **Chapter 10** – Jesus, The Good Shepherd
- **Chapter 11** – Jesus Raises Lazarus from the Dead
- **Chapter 12** – Jesus Enters Jerusalem
- **Chapter 13** – The Lord's Supper
- **Chapter 14** – Oneness with the Father
- **Chapter 15** – Jesus Is The Vine
- **Chapter 16** – The Promise of the Holy Spirit

- **Chapter 17** – Jesus's Intercessory Prayer
- **Chapter 18** – Judas Betrays Jesus
- **Chapter 19** – The Crucifixion of Jesus
- **Chapter 20** – The Empty Tomb
- **Chapter 21** – Jesus Appears to the Seven

Desserts

Needed: *Sharp Knife, Soup Spoon, and Salad Fork*

- Jesus (*the Word, the Son of God*)
- The Holy Spirit (*the Helper*)
- Rabboni (*Teacher*)
- John
- Thomas (*Didymus*)
- Judas Iscariot

Menu Lessons (Questions)

Since you have dined sufficiently on this meal, explain what you digested by answering the following questions:

1. How does John prove that Jesus is the Son of God and that believing you will have eternal life through his name?

2. What were some of the ways God's love was expressed through Jesus Christ?

3. List and explain the features of the seven "I Ams."

4.   What did Jesus teach in the gospel of John?

5.   The word *"believe"* was frequently repeated. List what you will receive if you believe in Christ.

Describe in your own words the savory flavors or sweet aromas that come from this meal.

* Describe your gourmet fine dining experience after you have learned that *Jesus is The Son of God.*

Here are some "After-Dinner Mints and Sweet Treats" (Promises and Blessings) for you to enjoy.
"Thank You for Dining with Us"

* *Whatever you ask in the name of Jesus, he will do so that the Father may be glorified in the Son*
* *The Holy Spirit (Helper) is with us forever*
* *Jesus came that we might have life and have it more abundantly*
* *Where Jesus is, there we will be also*
* *We have the right to become children of God when we receive him and believe in his name*
* *The Word (Jesus) dwelt among us, and we beheld his glory*
* *Whoever believes in Jesus has eternal life*

Compliments to the Master Chef

- *Praise God for all things came into being by him (John 1:3)*
- *Praise God for in Jesus is life and the life is the light of men (John 1:4)*
- *Praise God for the Son of God is King (John 1:49)*
- *Praise God, for he so loved the world that he gave his only begotten Son (John 3:16)*

ACTS

Sous Chef: Luke   *Date Meal Prepared: About AD 63*

Menu

The Royal Family Secret Ingredient:

Jesus is The Prince of Life

Your meal for today consists of becoming witnesses as we discover how the early Christians (followers of Christ) were led by the empowering of the Holy Spirit to spread the gospel of eternal life far beyond the boundaries of the Jewish culture to the whole world. The Lord never intended for his message to be confined to one small group of chosen people, the Israelites. The Prince of Life was fulfilling his promise to Abraham as foretold in the Old Testament in Genesis 12:1–3: "In you all the families of the earth shall be blessed."

1. Season your food with prayer and take your spiritual vitamins and supplements of praise and worship before you start eating your meal.

2. If necessary, review the Spiritual Fundamental Eating Concepts and Procedures for further instruction.

3. Pick a few *salads* you can put to memory to go along with some of the *entrées* you're going to dine on. Then, "pack a lunch for tomorrow" by writing them down on

an index card and putting the card in an index box to carry your favorite spiritual salads with you. Dine on them during your lunch break—feed both your physical and spiritual sides at the same time. Study and take note of all the ingredients in each salad you choose.

4. The Main House Salad (key verse) is listed under the salad menu below.

Appetizers

Needed: *Sharp Knife, Dinner Fork, and Salad Fork*

- Baptized with the Holy Spirit
- Receive Power
- Pentecost
- Utterance
- Persecution
- Filled with the Holy Spirit
- Speak with Other Tongues
- Angel of the Lord
- Fasting
- Apostles
- Spirit of Divination

Salad

Needed: *Sharp Knife, Dinner Fork, and Soup Spoon*

Suggested Main House Salad: Acts 1:8: "But you shall receive *power* when the Holy Spirit has come upon you; and you shall be *My Witnesses* both in Jerusalem and in all Judea and Samaria, and even to the *remotest* part of the earth."

Recipe for ACTS
Book Summary

Ingredients (Themes): *The indwelling and empowering activity of the Holy Spirit; the Kingdom of God; Forgiveness; Salvation; Christ's Return.*

The book of Acts covers approximately the first thirty years of the early church and was written to confirm the faith of believers. The apostles, especially Paul and Peter, were responsible through the empowering of the Holy Spirit for spreading Christianity from Jerusalem to Rome to the Jews and the Gentiles. The early believers took the gospel message to their cities, countries, and to the ends of the earth.

The revealing of the Holy Spirit was expressed as those who

believed in Christ Jesus received the gift of Jesus's Spirit. The Samaritans were also included along with the Gentiles in this gift of salvation. Salvation involved believers being filled with the Holy Spirit in order to live holy lives and be obedient to God's will, which was to spread the Word of God to the entire world.

Entrées

Needed: *Sharp Knife and Dinner Fork*

- **Chapter 1 –** The Ascension of Jesus Christ
- **Chapter 2 –** The Day of Pentecost
- **Chapter 3 –** Peter's Second Sermon and the Healing of a Lame Beggar
- **Chapter 4 –** The Imprisonment of Peter and John
- **Chapter 5 –** The Fate of Ananias and Sapphira
- **Chapter 6 –** The Appointment of the Seven
- **Chapter 7 –** Stephen's Martyrdom
- **Chapter 8 –** Saul's Persecution of the Church
- **Chapter 9 –** Saul's Conversion
- **Chapter 10 –** The Gospel Extended to the Gentiles
- **Chapter 11 –** The Church at Antioch
- **Chapter 12 –** Peter's Arrest and Deliverance
- **Chapter 13 –** Paul's First Missionary Journey
- **Chapter 14 –** Acceptance and Opposition
- **Chapter 15 –** The Council at Jerusalem and Paul's Second Missionary Journey
- **Chapter 16 –** The Second Missionary Journey
- **Chapter 17 –** Paul at Thessalonica, Berea, and Athens
- **Chapter 18 –** Paul at Corinth and His Third Missionary Journey

- **Chapter 19** – Paul at Ephesus
- **Chapter 20** – Paul in Macedonia and Greece
- **Chapter 21** – Paul's Journey to Jerusalem
- **Chapter 22** – Paul's Defense Before the Jews
- **Chapter 23** – The Council, the Conspiracy to Kill Paul, and Paul's Move to Caesarea
- **Chapter 24** – Paul before Felix
- **Chapter 25** – Paul before Festus and Agrippa
- **Chapter 26** – Paul's Defense before Agrippa
- **Chapter 27** – Paul Shipwrecked on His Way to Rome
- **Chapter 28** – Paul Arrives in Rome

Desserts
Needed: *Sharp Knife, Soup Spoon, and Salad Fork*

- Jesus (*Prince of Life*)
- The Holy Spirit
- Saul (*Paul*)
- Peter
- Cornelius
- Barnabas
- Lydia
- Ethiopian Eunuch
- Ananias and Sapphira

Menu Lessons (Questions)
Since you have dined sufficiently on this meal, explain what you digested by answering the following questions:

1. Why did Luke write the book of Acts?
2. What were some of the problems of the early church?

3. What were some of the activities of this active church?

Describe in your own words the savory flavors or sweet aromas that come from this meal.

- Describe your gourmet fine dining experience after you have learned that *Jesus is The Prince of Life*.

Here are some "After-Dinner Mints and Sweet Treats" (Promises and Blessings) for you to enjoy.
"Thank You for Dining with Us"

- *Jesus Christ is the Son of God*
- *God fills us with the Holy Spirit*
- *Everyone who believes in the name of Jesus receives forgiveness of sins*

Compliments to the Master Chef
- *Praise God for including the Gentiles in his salvation (Acts 4:12)*
- *Praise God that we can find him, for he is not far from each one of us (Acts 11:27)*
- *Praise God, for Jesus heals (Acts 9:34)*

ROMANS

Sous Chef: Paul   *Date Meal Prepared:* AD 56

Menu

The Royal Family Secret Ingredient:
Jesus is Our Righteousness

Your meal for today consists of unrighteous sinners receiving a right standing with God as a gift to justify their position in Christ. The righteousness of Christ was given to those who have faith in Jesus Christ, and it was justified through the death of Christ. For one to be justified before God, you must acknowledge that God's righteousness is upon yourself. In order to accomplish this, you must know God for yourself. Our knowledge of God is the same as the appropriation of the righteousness of God; it is resting on the mercy of God. The only way to God is through a personal relationship with Jesus Christ, through our faith and complete obedience to him alone. Through the righteousness of Jesus, we are no longer subject to condemnation.

1. Season your food with prayer and take your spiritual vitamins and supplements of praise and worship before you start eating your meal.

2. If necessary, review the Spiritual Fundamental Eating Concepts and Procedures for further instruction.

3. Pick a few *salads* you can put to memory to go along with some of the *entrées* you're going to dine on. Then, "pack a lunch for tomorrow" by writing them down on an index card and putting the card in an index box to carry your favorite spiritual salads with you. Dine on them during your lunch break—feed both your physical and spiritual sides at the same time. Study and take note of all the ingredients in each salad you choose.

4. The Main House Salad (key verse) is listed under the salad menu below.

Appetizers
Needed: *Sharp Knife, Dinner Fork, and Salad Fork*

- Righteousness
- Living by Faith
- Propitiation
- Adoption as Sons

- Living and Holy Sacrifice
- Justified
- Transformed
- Renewing of the Mind
- One Body in Christ
- Unrighteousness
- Transgression
- Bondage

Salad

Needed: *Sharp Knife, Dinner Fork and Soup Spoon*

Suggested Main House Salad: Romans 5:17: "For if by the transgression of the one, death *reigned* through the one, much more those who receive the abundance of grace and of the *gift of righteousness* will reign in life through the One, Jesus Christ."

Recipe for ROMANS
Book Summary

Ingredients (Themes): *Righteousness; Justification; God's Presence; The Holy Spirit.*

Paul shares with the Romans how as sinners believing in Christ Jesus, they are declared righteous and justified by faith to live a holy life before the Lord. Christ is presented as a descendant of David. God's provision of righteousness is revealed, and the fruit of righteousness is seen as a result in the saints of faith. We are all sinners in need of God's salvation. The full meaning of the cross of Jesus Christ is explained in Paul's statement, "For I am not ashamed of the gospel, for it is the power of God for salvation to everyone who believes" (Romans 1:16).

Entrées

Needed: *Sharp Knife and Dinner Fork*

- **Chapter 1 –** The Exalted Gospel
- **Chapter 2 –** The Impartiality of God
- **Chapter 3 –** All the World Is Guilty
- **Chapter 4 –** Justification of Old Testament Faith
- **Chapter 5 –** Results of Justification
- **Chapter 6 –** Believers Are Dead in Sin, Alive in God
- **Chapter 7 –** Believers United to Christ
- **Chapter 8 –** Deliverance from Bondage
- **Chapter 9 –** Solicitude for Israel
- **Chapter 10 –** The Word of Faith Brings Salvation
- **Chapter 11 –** Israel's Future Salvation
- **Chapter 12 –** Dedicated Service through a Transformed Life
- **Chapter 13 –** Obedience to Civil Law
- **Chapter 14 –** Judging One Another
- **Chapter 15 –** Self-Denial on Behalf of Others
- **Chapter 16 –** Greeting and Love Expressed

Desserts

Needed: *Sharp Knife, Soup Spoon, and Salad Fork*

- Paul
- Phoebe
- Prisca and Aquila

Menu Lessons (Questions)

Since you have dined sufficiently on this meal, explain what you digested by answering the following questions:

1. How are we made righteous and justified through Jesus Christ?
2. Does the Lord Jesus continue to take your sins into account?
3. What are the results of being justified by faith?

Describe in your own words the savory flavors or sweet aromas that come from this meal.

- Describe your gourmet fine dining experience after you have learned that *Jesus is Our Righteousness.*

Here are some "After-Dinner Mints and Sweet Treats" (Promises and Blessings) for you to enjoy.
"Thank You for Dining with Us"

- *We have peace with God through our Lord Jesus Christ*
- *We receive reconciliation to God through Jesus Christ*
- *We are justified by faith*
- *The Holy Spirit was given to us*

- *God demonstrated his own love toward us while we were yet sinners*

Compliments to the Master Chef

- *Praise God that the Spirit himself bears witness with our spirit that we are children of God (Romans 8:14)*
- *Praise God that his love has been poured out within our hearts through the Holy Spirit (Romans 5:5)*

1 CORINTHIANS

Sous Chef: Paul   *Date Meal Prepared*: About AD 52–53

Menu

The Royal Family Secret Ingredient:
Jesus is Our Gift

Your meal for today consists of learning about Christian conduct. When you become a Christian, your past practices of sinful behavior and conduct are not acceptable as a child of God. God will not tolerate sexual immorality and disorderly conduct causing divisions in the church. As Christians, we should be under the direction and influence of the Holy Spirit to conduct ourselves with wisdom, discernment, integrity, and faithfulness, whether inside or outside the church.

The importance of love is heavily expressed in this meal because it is the church's most effective gift and offensive weapon. Love is the very essence of God's nature and the most powerful force in the universe, and we have been given this powerful gift of love through Jesus Christ. Without love, all the various gifts of the Holy Spirit profit us nothing.

1. Season your food with prayer and take your spiritual vitamins and supplements of praise and worship before you start eating your meal.

2. If necessary, review the Spiritual Fundamental Eating Concepts and Procedures for further instruction.

3. Pick a few *salads* you can put to memory to go along with some of the *entrées* you're going to dine on. Then, "pack a lunch for tomorrow" by writing them down on an index card and putting the card in an index box to carry your favorite spiritual salads with you. Dine on them during your lunch break—feed both your physical and spiritual sides at the same time. Study and take note of all the ingredients in each salad you choose.

4. The Main House Salad (key verse) is listed under the salad menu below.

Appetizers
Needed: *Sharp Knife, Dinner Fork, and Salad Fork*

- Love
- The Lord's Supper
- Spiritual Gifts
- Prophecy
- Speaking in Tongues

- Men of Flesh (Carnal)
- Immorality
- Covetous
- Idolater

Salad

Needed: *Sharp Knife, Dinner Fork, and Soup Spoon*

Suggested Main House Salad: 1 Corinthians 13:2: "And if I have the gift of prophecy, and know all mysteries and all knowledge; and if I have all faith, so as to remove mountains, but do not have *love*, I am nothing."

Recipe for 1 CORINTHIANS
Book Summary

Ingredients (Themes): Morality; Spiritual Gifts;

Christian Unity; Marriage; Love; Strength; A Woman's Role in the Church.

Paul was on one of his missionary journeys, and this was his first canonical letter written to the Christians in Corinth. He believed that Corinth was a strategic center of influence because it had become one of the richest cities in the world.

Corinth was also full of sin and one of the wicked cities of ancient times. There were many religions represented with heathen and degrading customs of immorality, pagan temples, and religious prostitution. There were areas in the Corinthian church that needed correction and instruction because of the congregation's spiritual immaturity.

Many of the Corinthian Christians were recent converts from pagan practices and struggled with the adjustment to proper Christian conduct. There had risen in the church some very serious problems and disorders concerning gross immorality involving incestuous relationships, lawsuits between Christians in the presence of unbelievers, disorderly conduct at the worship assemblies, marital problems, and confusion as to women's roles in the church. There were also some heresies about the resurrection, abuses of the Lord's Supper, and difficulties with meat offerings to idols.

There had also been a brilliant display of spiritual gifts of the Holy Spirit. One spiritual gift was the speaking of tongues, which was very popular among the Corinthians. Everybody wanted this gift because people would look up to the person who possessed it. Some people even went to church just for the honor they would receive for themselves from displaying this gift.

Entrées

Needed: *Sharp Knife and Dinner Fork*

Desserts

Needed: *Sharp Knife, Soup Spoon, and Salad Fork*

- Risen Savior
- Apollos
- Maranatha

Menu Lessons (Questions)

Since you have dined sufficiently on this meal, explain what you digested by answering the following questions:

1. Why is love so important when exercising your spiritual gifts?
2. Why should you rely on the Holy Spirit now that he abides in you?
3. What happens when you judge someone else based on your standards?
4. Do you know your spiritual gift(s)?
5. Are you exercising your spiritual gift(s) while serving in your Father's house?

Describe in your own words the savory flavors or sweet aromas that come from this meal.

- Describe your gourmet fine dining experience after you have learned that *Jesus is Our Gift.*

Here are some "After Dinner-Mints and Sweet Treats" (Promises and Blessings) for you to enjoy.
"Thank You for Dining with Us"

- *We have the mind of Christ when we have the Holy Spirit*
- *We were washed, sanctified, and justified in the name of the Lord Jesus and in the Spirit of our God*
- *God will raise us up through his power*
- *We have been bought with a price*
- *If anyone loves God, he is known by him*
- *We were all made to drink of one Spirit*
- *Christ died for our sins according to the Scriptures*
- *We are enriched in Christ Jesus in all speech and all knowledge*
- *As saints, we can call upon the name of the Lord Jesus Christ*
- *We are not lacking in any gift*

Compliments to the Master Chef
- *Praise God for he is faithful (1 Corinthians 1:9 and 10:136)*
- *Praise God that we can boast in the Lord (1 Corinthians 1:31)*
- *Praise God that faith rests on the power of God (1 Corinthians 2:5)*
- *Praise God I can glorify him in my body (1 Corinthians 6:20)*
- *Praise God for there is but one God, the Father (1 Corinthians 8:46)*
- *Praise God for the earth is the Lord's and all it contains (1 Corinthians 10:26)*
- *Praise God because Christ is the head of every man (1 Corinthians 11:3)*
- *Praise God for love never fails (1 Corinthians 13:8a)*
- *Praise God for he is not a God of confusion but of peace, as in all the churches of the saints (1 Corinthians 14:33)*

1 CORINTHIANS

Sous Chef: Paul   ***Date Meal Prepared:** Between AD 55–57*

Menu

The Royal Family Secret Ingredient:
Jesus is Our Justification

Your meal for today consists of being made aware of certain errors, false teachings, and divisions that occur in the church. We have been instructed in our duty as Christians to handle church matters properly. Church leaders are to exercise discipline to keep order in the church. We must be loyal to Christ and not to human personalities. We are also to show generosity and support to those less fortunate than ourselves, especially our starving and poverty-stricken Christian brothers and sisters in Christ.

1. Season your food with prayer and take your spiritual vitamins and supplements of praise and worship before you start eating your meal.

2. If necessary, review the Spiritual Fundamental Eating Concepts and Procedures for further instruction.

3. Pick a few *salads* you can put to memory to go along with some of the *entrées* you're going to dine on. Then,

"pack a lunch for tomorrow" by writing them down on an index card and putting the card in an index box to carry your favorite spiritual salads with you. Dine on them during your lunch break—feed both your physical and spiritual sides at the same time. Study and take note of all the ingredients in each salad you choose.

4. The Main House Salad (key verse) is listed under the salad menu below.

Appetizers

Needed: *Sharp Knife, Dinner Fork, and Salad Fork*

- Be Made Complete
- Sealed Us
- Old Covenant
- New Covenant
- Transformed
- Darkness
- Reconciliation
- Apostleship
- Generosity
- Bound Together with Unbelievers

Salad

Needed: *Sharp Knife, Dinner Fork, and Soup Spoon*

Suggested Main House Salad: 2 Corinthians 5:15: "And He died for all, that they who *live* should no longer live for themselves, but for Him who died and *rose again* on their behalf."

Recipe for II CORINTHIANS
Book Summary

Ingredients (Themes): Freedom; Excellence; New Covenant; Justification; Generosity.

There were some leaders in the Corinthian church who were denying that Paul was a true apostle of Jesus, so Paul wrote this letter to vindicate himself. The letter to the Corinthian church was personal, with a strong undercurrent of defensiveness, because he refused to allow his apostolic authority and his ministry to be questioned. He was being attacked, and he was forced to justify his authority against these false leaders. He also wanted to confront his accusers who were disrupting his ministry work. Paul was defending his ministry against some false apostles who were trying to lead the Corinthians away from the gospel. He also wanted to remind the Corinthian Christians that because he had founded the church in Corinth, he did have the right to speak to them regarding the management and stewardship of the church.

Paul appealed to the Corinthians about their generosity. He requested that the churches he had founded give generous offerings to help the poor and starving Jewish Christian believers in Judea, which gave him an opportunity to teach the Corinthians about Christian stewardship and sacrificial giving. He also wanted to implement God's plan to eliminate the prejudices the Jews had against the Gentiles by showing them the Gentiles were truly their brothers and sisters in Christ because they financially supported them and genuinely loved them as God had commanded them to do toward one another.

Paul's letter included a discussion regarding the Old Covenant and the New Covenant. The Old Covenant was never intended to be permanent, because when Jesus Christ arrived, the New Covenant was intended to replace the Old Covenant with all its glory and benefits for the believer.

God showed his excellent love and generosity toward us by providing us with a New Covenant to show the richness of his love when he justified our righteousness through Jesus Christ.

Entrées

Needed: *Sharp Knife and Dinner Fork*

- **Chapter 1 –** Paul's Comfort in His Suffering
- **Chapter 2 –** Reaffirm Your Love
- **Chapter 3 –** Ministers of a New Covenant
- **Chapter 4 –** Paul's Living Martyrdom
- **Chapter 5 –** The Temporal and Eternal
- **Chapter 6 –** Their Ministry Commended
- **Chapter 7 –** Paul Reveals His Heart
- **Chapter 8 –** Great Generosity
- **Chapter 9 –** God Gives the Most
- **Chapter 10 –** Paul Describes Himself
- **Chapter 11 –** Paul Defends His Apostleship
- **Chapter 12 –** Paul's Vision and His Thorn in the Flesh
- **Chapter 13 –** Examine Yourselves

Desserts

Needed: *Sharp Knife, Soup Spoon, and Salad Fork*

- Paul (*True Apostle*)
- False Prophets

Menu Lessons (Questions)

Since you have dined sufficiently on this meal, explain what you digested by answering the following questions:

1. Why is church discipline necessary?
2. Generosity: Are you giving more than you are receiving?
3. Explain why it is so important to give more than to receive.

Describe in your own words the savory flavors or sweet aromas that come from this meal.

- Describe your gourmet fine dining experience after you have learned that *Jesus is Our Justification.*

Here are some "After-Dinner Mints and Sweet Treats" (Promises and Blessings) for you to enjoy
"Thank You for Dining with Us"

- *To Christ, we are presented as a pure virgin*
- *We have the grace of God*
- *We became the righteousness of God in him*
- *We are sons and daughters to God*
- *Our inner man is being renewed day by day*
- *We have a building from God, a house not made with hands, eternal in the heavens*
- *We are ambassadors for Christ*
- *We have an abundance of comfort through Christ*
- *We are established in Christ*
- *God has anointed and sealed us*
- *We have received the Spirit in our hearts as a pledge*

- *Our adequacy is from God*
- *We are adequate servants*

Compliments to the Master Chef

- *Praise God for being the Father of mercies and God of all comfort (2 Corinthians 1:3)*
- *Praise God who comforts us in all our afflictions (2 Corinthians 1:4)*
- *Praise God for being faithful (2 Corinthians 1:18a)*
- *Praise God, for all his promises are YES (2 Corinthians 1:20)*
- *Praise God for the sweet aroma of the knowledge of him in every place (2 Corinthians 2:14)*
- *Praise God for liberty (2 Corinthians 3:17)*
- *Praise God for the glory of the Lord (2 Corinthians 3:18)*
- *Praise God who reconciled us to himself through Christ (2 Corinthians 5:18)*
- *Praise God for the reconciliation of the world to himself (2 Corinthians 5:19a)*
- *Praise God for not counting our trespasses against us (2 Corinthians 5:19b)*
- *Praise God who knew no sin, that he was made to be sin on our behalf (2 Corinthians 5:21)*
- *Praise God for the day of salvation (2 Corinthians 6:2)*
- *Praise God who dwells in us and walks among us (2 Corinthians 6:16a)*
- *Praise God, for he is our God and we are his people (2 Corinthians 6:16b)*
- *Praise God, for he is a Father to us (2 Corinthians 6:18)*
- *Praise God for his godly jealousy for us (2 Corinthians 11:2)*
- *Praise God, for Jesus is blessed forever (2 Corinthians 11:31)*

HEBREWS

Sous Chef: Possibly Paul   *Date Meal Prepared:* AD 70

Menu

The Royal Family Secret Ingredient:
Jesus is My Intercessor

Your meal for today consists of learning that Jesus Christ provided a better way of life through our faith in him when he interceded for us by making a better sacrifice and offering a better covenant than all of the old dead sacrifices and the Old Covenant could provide. He is found to be better than Moses, Joshua, the angels, and all of the high priests of old because he intercedes as a Living Sacrifice. Our faith in Jesus Christ is secure because as an Intercessor, Jesus has cleared the way for us to have direct access to the throne of God.

1. Season your food with prayer and take your spiritual vitamins and supplements of praise and worship before you start eating your meal.

2. If necessary, review the Spiritual Fundamental Eating Concepts and Procedures for further instruction.

3. Pick a few *salads* you can put to memory to go along with some of the *entrées* you're going to dine on. Then, "pack a lunch for tomorrow" by writing them down on an index card and putting the card in an index box to carry your favorite spiritual salads with you. Dine on them during your lunch break—feed both your physical and spiritual sides at the same time. Study and take note of all the ingredients in each salad you choose.

4. The Main House Salad (key verse) is listed under the salad menu below.

Appetizers
Needed: *Sharp Knife, Dinner Fork, and Salad Fork*

- Intercessor
- New Covenant
- Draw Near
- By Faith

Salad
Needed: *Sharp Knife, Dinner Fork, and Soup Spoon*

Suggested Main House Salad: Hebrews 1:3: "And He is the radiance of His glory and the *exact representation* of His

nature, and upholds all things by the word of His power. When He had made purification of sins, He sat down at the right hand of the Majesty on high."

Recipe for HEBREWS
Book Summary

Ingredients (Themes): *Christ Intercedes; The New Covenant; Christ's Priesthood; Salvation.*

The apostle Paul wanted to explain that the zealousness of offering animal sacrifices was no longer of any significance because the animals could never take away sin. Now that Christ has come, animal blood was no longer necessary because the blood of the Lamb of God is now the only blood that continually takes away sin.

Paul wanted to free the Hebrews from the ceremonies of the law, which they were very fond of performing. He needed to persuade them to adhere to the Christian faith and persevere in it.

Entrées
Needed: *Sharp Knife and Dinner Fork*

- **Chapter 1** – God's Final Word in His Son

- **Chapter 2 –** Christ's Unity with Man
- **Chapter 3 –** Jesus, Our High Priest
- **Chapter 4 –** The Believer's Rest
- **Chapter 5 –** The Perfect High Priest
- **Chapter 6 –** Warning Against Apostasy
- **Chapter 7 –** The Order of Melchizedek
- **Chapter 8 –** The New Covenant
- **Chapter 9 –** The Old and the New
- **Chapter 10 –** One Sacrifice of Christ Is Sufficient
- **Chapter 11 –** Heroes of Faith
- **Chapter 12 –** Jesus, the Perfect Example
- **Chapter 13 –** The Changeless Christ

Desserts
Needed: *Sharp Knife, Soup Spoon, and Salad Fork*
- Jesus (*High Priest*)
- Melchizedek

Menu Lessons (Questions)
Since you have dined sufficiently on this meal, explain what you digested by answering the following questions:

1. Why was the word **"better"** served twelve times in this meal?
2. What was "better" or superior about the New Covenant over the Old Covenant?
3. What were the list of instructions given to every prince and princess in chapter 13?

Describe in your own words the savory flavors or sweet aromas that come from this meal.

- Describe your gourmet fine dining experience after you have learned that *Jesus is My Intercessor.*

Here are some "After-Dinner Mints and Sweet Treats" (Promises and Blessings) for you to enjoy.
"Thank You for Dining with Us"

- *We are equipped in every good thing to do the Father's will*
- *God puts his love upon our hearts*
- *God will not remember our sins and lawless deeds*
- *Jesus offered himself as a sacrifice for all!*
- *Jesus is our God, and we are his people*
- *Jesus entered as a Forerunner for us*
- *Jesus has become the guarantee of a better covenant for us*
- *Jesus is able to save forever those who* draw near to God *through him*

Compliments to the Master Chef
- *Praise God for making us partakers of the Holy Spirit (Hebrews 6:4)*
- *Praise God, for it is* impossible *for him to lie (Hebrews 6:18)*
- *Praise God, for "thou art a priest forever according to the order of Melchizedek" (Hebrews 7:17)*
- *Praise God because Jesus abides forever and he holds his priesthood permanently (Hebrews 7:24)*
- *Praise God that Christ's appearance as a High Priest is a sign of the good things to come (Hebrews 9:11a)*
- *Praise God, for he has provided something better for us (Hebrews 11:40)*
- *Praise God and give thanks to his name (Hebrews 13:15)*

REVELATION

Sous Chef: John   *Date Meal Prepared: Between AD 81–96*

Menu

The Royal Family Secret Ingredient:
Jesus is Alpha and Omega

Your Meal for today consists of discovering the unveiling revelation of the First and the Last and what the future holds for the church during the grand finale of history in the ultimate triumph of the Second Coming of the Lord to destroy all evil. The meal uncovers the sinfulness of humans and the outcome of those who choose to follow the Lamb receiving blessings and those who choose to follow the beast receiving eternal damnation. We are reminded that Jesus Christ is "King of kings and Lord of lords" and that he will soon return. Our steadfast faith will be vindicated because Satan will be destroyed forever.

1. Season your food with prayer and take your spiritual vitamins and supplements of praise and worship before you start eating your meal.

2. If necessary, review the Spiritual Fundamental Eating Concepts and Procedures for further instruction.

3. Pick a few *salads* you can put to memory to go along with some of the *entrées* you're going to dine on. Then, "pack a lunch for tomorrow" by writing them down on an index card and putting the card in an index box to carry your favorite spiritual salads with you. Dine on them during your lunch break—feed both your physical and spiritual sides at the same time. Study and take note of all the ingredients in each salad you choose.

4. The Main House Salad (key verse) is listed under the salad menu below.

Appetizers
Needed: *Sharp Knife, Dinner Fork, and Salad Fork*

- Revelation
- I Am the *First* and the *Last*
- Alpha and Omega
- Prophecy
- Angels
- Holy
- Tree of Life
- Amen
- Seven

- New Heaven and New Earth
- Keys of Death and of Hades
- Babylon
- Isle of Patmos
- Bond Servant
- Tribulation
- Testimony

Salad

Needed: *Sharp Knife, Dinner Fork, and Soup Spoon*

Suggested Main House Salad: Revelation 1:8: "I am the *Alpha* **and the** *Omega,* **says the Lord God, who is and who was and who is to come, the Almighty."**

Recipe for REVELATION
Book Summary

Ingredients (Themes): The Almighty Ultimate Triumphal Return; The Lamb's Victory; Prophecy; God's Wrath Against Sin; Freedom; Hope.

John was banished to the Isle of Patmos to prophesy the whole period of church history to the end of the world. He unfolded the future of the church's struggles to its final victory. John talks about "things which are," that were in his day in the seven letters to the seven churches, dealing with their situation as it was then, and "things which shall be hereafter." This covers the time from then on to the end.

The Apostle Christ will reward the righteous and judge the wicked. John writes "the time is at hand" to express a sense of urgency.

Entrées
Needed: *Sharp Knife and Dinner Fork*

- **Chapter 1 –** The Revelation of Jesus Christ and Things to Come
- **Chapter 2 –** Church Messages to Ephesus, Smyrna, Pergamum and Thyatira
- **Chapter 3 –** Church Messages to Sardis, Philadelphia, and Laodicea
- **Chapter 4 –** Scenes from Heaven and the Throne of God
- **Chapter 5 –** The Book with Seven Seals
- **Chapter 6 –** The Opening of Six Seals
- **Chapter 7 –** The 144,000 and the Great Multitude in Heaven
- **Chapter 8 –** The Seventh Seal Opened
- **Chapter 9 –** The Fifth and Sixth Trumpet
- **Chapter 10 –** The Angel and the Little Book
- **Chapter 11 –** Two Witnesses and the Seventh Trumpet
- **Chapter 12 –** The Women, the Child, and the Dragon
- **Chapter 13 –** The Beast from the Sea and the Earth

Desserts
Needed: *Sharp Knife, Soup Spoon, and Salad Fork*

- Jesus (*the Lamb; the Christ; the King of kings and Lord of lords*)
- The Almighty
- John
- The Beast
- The False Prophet
- Prince of the devil

Menu Lessons (Questions)

Since you have dined sufficiently on this meal, explain what you digested by answering the following questions:

1. List the characteristics of the seven churches (positive and negative):

   • Evaluate each church by listing things that are repeated, emphasized, related, true to life, alike and unlike.

   • Study each church, person, and place mentioned to see if it will shed some light on the meal as a whole.

2. What issues does this spiritual meal address?

3. What have you tasted in this spiritual meal that challenges the way you live?

Explain from your dining experience the sweet aromas and savory flavors that come from the Lamb as:

   • **The Lion of the Tribe of Judah** *(Revelation 5:15)*

   • **The Word of God** *(Revelation 19:13)*

   • **King of Kings and Lord of Lords** *(Revelation 19:16)*

   • **The Beginning and the End** *(Revelation 22:13)*

Describe in your own words the savory flavors or sweet aromas that come from this meal.

- Describe your gourmet fine dining experience after you have learned that *Jesus is Alpha and Omega.*

Here are some "After-Dinner Mints and Sweet Treats" (Promises and Blessings) for you to enjoy.
"Thank You for Dining with Us"

- *God loves us and released us from our sins by his blood*
- *Jesus has made us to be kingdom priests to his God and Father*
- *We are clothed in white robes*

Compliments to the Master Chef

- *Praise God for the One who is and who was and who is to come (Revelation 1:4)*
- *Praise God, for Jesus Christ is the Faithful Witness (Revelation 1:5)*
- *Praise God for his glory and dominion forever and ever (Revelation 1:6)*
- *Praise God, for he is the Alpha and the Omega (Revelation 1:8a)*
- *Praise God the Almighty (Revelation 1:8b)*
- *Praise God for his Word and the testimony of Jesus (Revelation 1:9)*
- *Praise God, for he is holy who is True (Revelation 2:7)*
- *Praise God, for worthy is the Lamb who was slain (Revelation 5:1)*

Chapter 8

A Special Meal Prepared for Salvation

Scripture: 1 Peter 2:2
"Like <u>newborn babes</u>, long for the <u>pure milk</u> of the <u>word</u>,
that by it you may grow in respect to salvation,
if you have <u>tasted</u> the kindness of the Lord."

A Special Meal Prepared for Salvation
The Recipe for Salvation

This portion of the menu has been prepared for believers to share with all those who are not saved. They are not safe without "the Meal of Salvation." You must be born again in order to enjoy the meals that have been prepared for all of the King's kids.

Sin has separated the sinner from the King, the God who created us, and the only way back to him is to go through his Son, Jesus Christ. It is time for the unsaved to stop dining with Satan, the devil, and to dine with the King by feasting on the Living Word. In order to dine at the King's banquet table, everyone must receive the extended invitation by accepting the Son of God, Jesus Christ, as personal Lord and Savior. God has a wonderful plan for every life.

If you desire to experience the full and meaningful abundance of life by inheriting all the promises and blessings given to every child of God, then you must surrender your will unto the King. You can do this by faith as you repeat this simple prayer.

If you are already saved, please spend a few moments to share this prayer with those outside the kingdom of God so that they too will be filled with the Aged Royal Wine of the Holy Spirit and receive a blessing for eternity.

PRAYER

"Lord, I need you. Thank you for dying on the cross for my sins. Please forgive me. I open the door to my heart and receive you as my personal Lord and Savior. Thank you for forgiving me of my sins and giving me eternal life. Now take control of my life and make me the kind of person you want me to be. In Jesus's name I pray, Amen."

If you have prayed this prayer out loud to be saved, you are now born again, and God now considers you one of his children. I encourage you, as a new believer in Christ, to continue praying and reading the Bible every day. Ask God to lead you to a Bible-teaching church where you can be surrounded by your newly adopted brothers and sisters in Christ and grow into a strong and healthy Christian.

The King and all of his children rejoice and welcome our newly adopted brother or sister in Christ into the holy family of God. Now that you are in the holy family of God, please take a seat at the banquet table and dine on the Word of God until your heart is content.

Welcome to the Family, and God Bless You,
Sweet Prince or Princess!
LONG LIVE THE KING OF OUR SALVATION!

Chapter 9

Creating Your Own Spiritual Recipes

Scripture: 2 Timothy 2:15
"_Study_ to show thyself _approved_ unto God, a workman that has nothing to be ashamed of, _rightly dividing_ the word of truth."

Study Forms

Word and Term Study
Verse-To-Verse Study
Character Study
Chapter Study (Analysis)
Outlining the Principal Features of the Meal
Your Daily Bread Spiritual Journal

You create your own Spiritual Recipes by using the Study Forms. This is your opportunity to use the various study forms when your royal dinner is served. You can record all the wonderful discoveries from your dining experiences as you feast on each spiritual meal prepared by the Master Chef.

WORD AND TERM STUDY

"Test all things; hold fast what is good."
— 1 Thessalonians 5:21

Word/Term:

_____

Scripture Reference:

_____

Resource Tool (Sharp Knife, Dinner and Salad Forks) : Use the Bible Dictionary and the Concordance to find out how the word or term is used in the selected passage of scripture.

The Original Meaning of the Word/Term:

_____
_____
_____
_____
_____

How is it used in the text?

_____
_____
_____
_____
_____

Translation Comparison: How Is the Word Used in Other Bible Translations?

Bible Translation:

_____
_____

Meaning:

_____
_____
_____
_____
_____
_____

Bible Translation:

_____

Meaning:

_____
_____
_____
_____
_____
_____

Dictionary Meaning:

_____
_____
_____
_____
_____
_____
_____

VERSE-TO-VERSE STUDY

"Your word I have hidden in my heart, That I might not sin
against Thee."
— *Psalm 119:11*

*Resource Tool (Sharp Knife, Dinner Fork and Dinner Spoon) : Use
the concordance and the commentary to gain a greater knowledge
and clearer understanding of the verse(s) you selected to study.*

Suggestion:
- Pay close attention to the verses that are ahead of and behind each verse you are studying.
- Compare verses by examining parallel passages of Scripture that give an account of the same event.
- Revisit the verse over and over again until you have gotten as much as you possibly can get out of it. Write down everything that is revealed to you as you dine on the Word.
- Keep a list of unanswered questions and unresolved issues for further study.

Verse:

_____

_____

A. What does this verse mean?

_____

_____

_____

_____

_____

_____

_____

B. What does this verse teach me?

_____

_____

_____

_____

_____

_____

_____

_____

C. What are my questions and/or issues with this verse?

_____

_____

_____

_____

_____

_____

D. What are the answers to my questions and/or unresolved issues?

_____

_____

_____

_____

_____

_____

_____

_____

_____

_____

CHAPTER STUDY

*"Be diligent to present yourself approved to God, a workman
who does not need to be ashamed,
rightly dividing the word of truth"*
— 2 Timothy 2:15

Passage of Scripture: _____

Resource Tool (Sharp Knife)

Instructions:
- Identify the main idea or theme of the chapter, and then state it in a couple of words. Evaluate how the chapter, as a whole, relates to the rest of the book.
- Answer the following questions. *Focus on contrasts, similarities (words that are either opposite or similar to each other), and things that are repeated, related, emphasized, or true to the experiences of your own life.*

5. What does it say about Christ, and what name is used to describe Him in this chapter?

_____
_____
_____
_____

6. Who is speaking, who are they speaking to, and what is the reason or circumstance behind this chapter?

_____
_____
_____
_____

7. What are the main promises (if any) and what conditions are required to obtain these promises?

_____

_____

_____

_____

8. Are there any commands or instructions to follow?

_____

_____

_____

_____

9. Are there any errors made or sins committed that
    should be avoided?

_____

_____

_____

_____

10. What have I observed in this chapter that challenges
    the way I live today?

_____

_____

_____

11. What do I need from this chapter to apply to my life
    today?

_____

_____

_____

12. Was there a prayer in this chapter that I need to echo?

_____

_____

_____

_____

THE ROYAL CANDLELIGHT AND YOU
10 Recipes for Godly Living
CHARACTER STUDY

"For the LORD gives wisdom; from His mouth comes knowledge and understanding."
— *Proverbs 2:6*

Resource Tool: Study Bible (Sharp Knife), Commentary (Dinner Spoon) and Handbook (Salad Fork)

Name of Character: _____

Scripture Reference: _____

- What is the meaning of this character's name?

  _____
  _____
  _____
  _____
  _____
  _____
  _____

- Does the meaning of this character's name have any bearing on the passage of Scripture or the theme of the book?

  _____
  _____
  _____
  _____
  _____
  _____
  _____
  _____
  _____
  _____

- What are the elements of power and success that this character possesses or experiences?

_____
_____
_____
_____
_____
_____
_____

- Does this character experience any elements of suffering, weakness, or failure? If so, what are they?

_____
_____
_____
_____
_____
_____
_____
_____

- Were there any difficulties this character had to overcome? If so, why?

_____
_____
_____
_____
_____
_____
_____
_____

- Do I see a type of Christ in this character? (That is, does this character show any characteristics of Jesus Christ?)

  _____

  _____

  _____

  _____

  _____

  _____

  _____

- Was this character obedient or disobedient to God? What were the consequences of the character's actions (good or bad)?

  _____

  _____

  _____

  _____

  _____

  _____

  _____

- Did this character commit a sin, neglect any opportunities presented, or make any mistakes that I need to take into consideration when examining his or her actions?

  _____

  _____

  _____

  _____

  _____

_____
_____
_____
_____
_____

- What have I learned from this character that will help me in my relationship with Christ?

_____
_____
_____
_____
_____
_____
_____
_____
_____
_____
_____
_____

"Remember those who led you who spoke the word of God to you; and considering the result of their conduct, imitate their faith."
Hebrews 13:7 (NASB)

OUTLINING THE PRINCIPAL FEATURES OF YOUR STUDY
Completing Your Meal

"All scripture is given by inspiration of God, and is profitable for doctrine, for reproof, for correction, for instruction in righteousness."
— *2 Timothy 3:16*

NAME OF THE BOOK (The Meal):

_____

THEME (Main Features of the Meal) in one or two words or a phrase:

_____
_____
_____
_____

MAJOR POINTS (Qualities of the Meal): What practical issues does this book address?

- _____
- _____
- _____
- _____
- _____
- _____

THE CONCLUSION (Observation): What have I seen in this book?

_____

_____

_____

_____

_____

MY DINING EXPERIENCE (Interpretation): Personal Insight:

_____

_____

_____

_____

_____

SINS TO AVOID (Weight-Loss Program): What have I seen that challenges the way I live?

_____

_____

_____

_____

_____

PERSONAL LIFE-CHANGING APPLICATION (Healthy Dietary Program): What changes do I need to consider in light of this study?

_____

_____

_____

_____

Note: Share the results of your study with someone you love.

THE ROYAL CANDLELIGHT AND YOU
10 Recipes for Godly Living

YOUR DAILY BREAD SPIRITUAL JOURNAL

"I have treasured the words of His mouth more than my necessary food."
— Job 23:12

Scripture _____

Date: _____

List the Royal Candlelight message you received from God today:

_____
_____
_____
_____
_____

List the After-Dinner Mint or Sweet Treat (Promise or Blessing) from God you were given:

_____
_____
_____
_____
_____

List the Condition that must be met to receive an After-Dinner Mint or Sweet Treat:

_____
_____
_____
_____
_____

_____

List the Command(s) to Keep:

_____
_____
_____
_____
_____
_____
_____

List the Timeless Principle(s) you see in this passage:

_____
_____
_____
_____
_____
_____
_____

List Applications to your life (Exercise Program):

_____
_____
_____
_____
_____
_____
_____

Write Out Your Vitamins and Supplements (Praise and Worship Report):

_____
_____
_____
_____
_____
_____
_____
_____
_____

SPIRITUAL CULINARY VOCABULARY GLOSSARY

Votives of Light

Scripture: John 8:31-32
"If you abide in My word,
then you are truly disciples of Mine;
and you shall know the truth,
and the truth shall make you free."

Spiritual Culinary Vocabulary Glossary

The Vocabulary that is listed is culinary terms or allegory that will be used in all five (5) Spiritual Recipe Books for godly living.

After Dinner Mints – The promises that we receive from The King and The Master Chef, Jesus Christ, to say *"Thank You for Dining with Us"*.

Appetizers – *Words and terms* used in the Bible that stimulates the appetite.

Bitter Herbs – Bad characteristics that are disagreeable, distasteful, or distressing leading to the pain and suffering of a prince or princess of the King.

Bon Appétit – French term that means "I Wish You a Hearty Appetite!"

Bon Jour – French term that means "Hello".

Bowl of Stew for Damnation (*STEW – Souls Tasting Eternal Wrath*) A special dish of leftovers prepared by the Master Chef which contains the anger and wrath of God for all those who chose to hate and reject His Son, Jesus Christ. This meal has all the ingredients from the bitter herbs and spices of wickedness, sin, evil, disobedience and rebellion; along with a cup of wine of His bitter fury added to enhance the flavor of God's hatred of sin and immorality.

BYOB – *("Bring Your Own Bible")* Good practice to carry your own bible so you can read from it at church and study from it at home.

Calorie Desserts – Characters that possess bad qualities or characteristics and produced sin in their life by being disobedient to The King.

CHEW – Christians Having Eternal Wealth.

Chewing – Taking the necessary time to meditate on the Word of God.

Compliments to the Master Chef – Praises and words of gratitude to express your appreciation of the meals and what you tasted and experienced from the Master Chef that was good for you and to you.

Cuisine – The manner of preparing spiritual food.

Culinary Allegories – Extended metaphors that are used to demonstrate or express great truths through symbols or objects illustrated in this spiritual recipe book to teach or explain an idea or truth about human conduct or experiences.

Cup of Soup for Salvation – The passage of Scripture (John 3:16) that gives the unsaved soul a message of salvation that was specially prepared by the Master Chef to warm the heart and invite the sinner to repent and accept Jesus Christ as their Lord and Savior.

De Jour – French term that means *"of or from the day,"* it also means special to that day.

Decorum – Good behavior, or taste in conduct that adheres to customs and polite manners with a godly fear of offending The King.

Desserts – A course of *characters* in the Bible served at the close of a spiritual meal.

Dietary Fiber of Knowledge – The necessary nutritional information required for your complete spiritual growth.

Digesting – Gaining an understanding of the word of God by thinking over and arranging systematically in the mind; to comprehend.

Dining/Eating – To feed on the Word of God through reading; to take or consume by studying the Word of God.

Entrees – The main courses of study, that is, *chapters* in the Bible.

Etiquette – Table manners that govern your conduct in observance to The King's rules when spiritually eating. This includes the appropriate use of spiritual silverware/utensils.

Exercise Program/Exercising – Personal application and practices of the Word of God that involves love, faith, obedience, forgiveness, prayer, and using your spiritual gifts.

Fat Free Desserts – Characters that possess good qualities and characteristics that contain no form of sin.

Fat/Trans Fat – The sin in one's life that causes spiritual heart disease or spiritual death.

Feast – An elaborate meal, or banquet, of spiritual food that gives an unusual abundance of pleasure.

Fine Dining – Reading and studying the word of God to gain a higher level of spiritual maturity.

Flavors – A savory blend of predominant qualities in the characteristics of a believer that distinguishes him or her from those outside the family of God—that is, the "Fruit of the Spirit" listed in Galatians 5. The flavors consist of joy, peace, patience, kindness, goodness, faithfulness, gentleness, and self-control.

Free Radicals of Temptation – The sinful schemes Satan uses to attack the weak parts of the spiritual body's immune system. They are unstable and highly reactive and can damage the spiritual body because they accelerate the progression of spiritual cancer cells and cardiovascular diseases that affect the heart.

Generation to Generation – The way in which biblical instructions were passed down from Genesis to Revelation.

Great Recipe Book – The sacred Scriptures of the Bible, comprised of Old and New Testaments.

"God, You & I" Dance – *("G" "U" and "I" Dance)* Guidance; to perform rhythmic guiding movements provided by God, who leads and directs us His way in order to properly direct you through this life. *(Very Special Treat – "Steppin' In The Name of The Lord")*

Healthy Dietary Program – A compilation of the impressive good qualities and characteristics of those in the Bible; a list of those life changing behaviors, attitudes, habits, personalities, characteristics, and practices that will enhance your life if emulated.

Ingredients – The main theme or themes of a chapter.

Just Say "NO NO" – The "No Bible, No Breakfast" rule that should be practiced every morning to ensure we feed our spiritual bodies before we feed our physical bodies.

Main House Salad – This is the suggested main verse in the chapter to help summarize the theme.

Marinate – To soak in what you have learn to enrich the flavor of the Word.

Master Chef – Jesus Christ, who is the Head, who holds the authority and skills to teach and spiritually guide and directed, and who directed those used to assist in preparing the sixty-six meals of the Bible.

Master Meal Plan – Jesus' plan for us to spend eternity with Him.

Meals – The sixty-Six books of the Bible.

Menu – An overview of what today's authentic Christian can expect to find dealing with certain issues in a particular book selected to read and study.

Menu Lessons – A list of questions served after a spiritual meal to gain spiritual knowledge and maturity.

Mise en Place – The process used to arrange or prepare for studying the Word of God.

Pack A Lunch – A place (Index Box) where your recorded "memory verses" of Scripture are written on index cards and stored to refer to and dine on while dining on your physical lunch.

Personally Prescribed Spiritual Vitamins & Vitamin Supplements – The essential substances of *praise* and *worship* that provides energy to building up your spiritual immune system.

Prince – A male member of the royal family of God and the son of The King, noble in rank and status.

Princess – A female member of the royal family of God and the daughter of The King, outstanding and possesses the beautiful quiet spirit that The King honors.

Recipe of Meals – A summary of the books in the Bible.

Royal Attire – The Full Armor of God, a garment of spiritually fine white linen made of faith and love, to be worn by the prince and princess as they go about their day to protect them against evil and the Evil One. The six-piece attire is:

1. **Belt of Truth** – To practice a life of honesty and truthfulness.

2. **Breastplate of Righteousness** – The righteous character and deeds of the believer, which are full of faith and love.

3. **Feet Shod** – The preparation of the gospel of peace, which is the firm foundation, which are to stand on to spread the gospel.

4. **Shield of Faith** – God's protection against all the attacks of our spiritual enemy, Satan.

5. **Helmet of Salvation** – A crown of wisdom and discernment that represents the mind of Christ and carries an engraving that says *"Holiness to the Lord"*.

6. **Sword of the Spirit** – The Word of God, the offensive weapon used to combat all of Satan's lies.

Royal Candlelight – Jesus Christ is the special Light centered on The King's banquet table, considered while dining on a spiritual meal.

Royal Candlelight Devotional Moments – Sitting daily before the presence of The King to read one or two chapters of the Bible, preferably in the mornings before you start your busy day.

Royal Court – The church and the kingdom of God.

Royalty – The special characteristics of the prince and princess that are peculiar but acceptable in conduct, speech, and appearance in representing The King. They are of superior status, power and position and have a privileged class of kingly ancestry with high ranks and high standing.

Salads – Individual *verses* in the Bible.

Seasoning – To converse with or address God in prayer to enhance the natural flavors of His word and make it palatable to us in order to taste and see that the Lord is good.

Side Dishes – Instructions to help remind you of what is necessary to fully enjoy the meal before you start to dine.

Soul Food Menus – Instructions prepared from the heart of the Master Chef, Jesus Christ in which God expressed His love for us.

Sous Chefs – The apostles, prophets, evangelists, pastors and teachers: the authors, with various cultural backgrounds, of the sixty-six books of the Bible.

Special Treats – The unique way of studying God's Word that will bring unexpected joy and delight to the soul.

Spices – The love that God uses in His Word, giving zest to all its spiritual ingredients.

Spiritual A La Carte – The Spiritual Gourmet Chef's Spiritual Menu of actual individual dishes prepared for your physical dining pleasure that is listed separately from God's Menu and Dishes.

Spiritual Connoisseurs – Spiritual culinary professionals who are not ashamed of the gospel, but use their spiritual gifts to spread the gospel and build up the body of Christ.

Spiritual Culinary Skills – Spiritual gifts that are given to you by the Holy Spirit.

Spiritual Dinner Table – The special place where you choose to study the Word of God.

Spiritual Food – Truths, teachings, and principles relating to sacred matters that nourish, sustain, guide and supply the spiritual body.

Spiritual Food Borne Illnesses – The spiritual viruses, parasites, and bacteria that Satan has control over and uses to contaminate and attack every believer of God's word. *(Ephesians 6:12)*

Spiritual Maturity – The personal, spiritual characteristics of a mature Christian due to his or her continued spiritual growth by studying and applying the Word of God.

Spiritual Proteins – The natural components found in the Word of God that God provides for His children to guarantee their holiness and righteousness in Him.

Spiritual Utensils – The resource tools used to successfully study the Word of God. The five-piece spiritual flatware is:

Sharp Knife – Study Bible

Dinner Fork – Concordance

Salad Forks – Bible Dictionary and Bible Encyclopedia

Soup Spoon – Commentary

Dessert Fork – Handbook

Spiritual Breakfast Bar or Snack – Reading one or two chapters in the Bible every morning.

Spiritual Vegetables and Fruits – Verses of scripture that include parables, miracles, prayers, events and the Lord's conversations with people.

STEW – *Souls Tasting Eternal Wrath.* A meal prepared for Damnation.

Stock – The foundation used to create the base in each meal.

Swallowing – Understanding God's Word by absorbing what you have meditated upon and accepting the word of truth without question, protest or resentment.

Sweet Herbs – The compassion that God uses to bring out the genuine qualities expressed in His Word.

Sweet Treats – The blessings we receive from The King and the Master Chef, Jesus Christ, to say to us *"Thank You for Dining with Us."*

Table Manners – The proper way in which we are to dine at The King's table.

Taste – Various levels of understanding.

The King – God, who is the Ruler of life and His heavenly kingdom.

The Lamb – Jesus Christ, the special main secret ingredient used as the foundational stock, used in every meal, showing the tender, sweet, dear and gentle sacrificial parts of our Lord and Savior.

The Aged Royal Wine *(Special Fruit Drink)* – The Holy Spirit, who is the active presence of God in human life, constituting the Third Person of the Trinity. We should spiritually drink of the Holy Spirit everyday for spiritual guidance and direction to assist us in our obedience towards The King.

The Royal Family Main Secret Ingredient – The various characteristics of Jesus Christ demonstrated in each book of the Bible.

Weight Loss Program – Life-changing application based on our own list of sins of those committed by the characters in the Bible, as well as our own personal sins that we have learned of that offends the King and needs to be eliminated from our spiritual body.

Vol-Au-Dent of Fruit – Spiritual puff pastry filled with specially prepared characters, who were perfectly fruitful in their obedient to God.

Yeast – Self-rising traces of pride or arrogance, causing haughty behaviors that makes the believer appear "puffed up" in his or her attitude, which is displeasing and destructive because of selfish motives and attitudes toward God and others.

Note: **Yeast or leaven is a Biblical symbol of sin.**

The Author
Your Spiritual Gourmet Chef
of
The Royal Candlelight and You

Lynn Williams is a Certified Gourmet Chef with a Culinary Arts Degree in French cooking; receiving her college degree in culinary arts and hotel management. Her college education extends to floral and interior designing and decoration. She is the co-founder of The Royal Candlelight Publishing Co. Her career has been established as an author, workshop presenter, bible study teacher at The Teleois Institute and Ministry Director for the Vacation Bible School, Events Planning, Fitly Joined and the Political Awareness ministries at Ecclesia Christian Fellowship, located in San Bernardino, California; one of California's well known churches in the community and in the Inland Empire.

Lynn has owned her catering, floral designing, wedding and events planning business for 29 years. She has also developed her own line of Christian books called "The Royal Candlelight Christian Book Series." The series of books are being developed to point you to the truth, which can only be found in the word of God. Five of the books will be spiritual culinary recipe books written in culinary allegory based on all 66 Books of the Bible. The other line of Christian books will be based on life experiences and various life situations written in allegory to encourage the true believer of God by assisting them in finding the truth about what God has to say about their life challenges according to the governing principles of His word.

Lynn is dedicated to humbly serving God and His people by taking every opportunity to minister, love and cater to *"picking up the broken pieces in the lives of believers."*

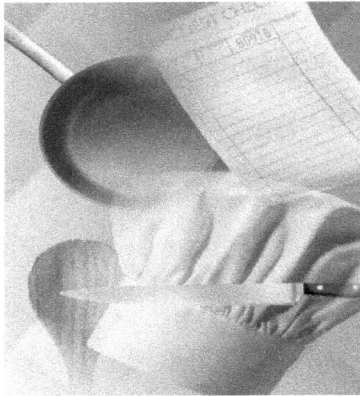

ROYAL CANDLELIGHT CHRISTIAN PUBLISHING COMPANY

ADVERTISEMENTS

God makes His presence known to us, and we have an awesome opportunity to experience His presence everyday while growing into a deep, intimate relationship with God. To help us do that, Lynn Williams has created a way for us to spend more time with God as you learn how to study the Bible in this very unique and enjoyable way.

Whether you use the Royal Candlelight study guides or read the Bible on your own, once you've completed the "meals" of God's Word by studying them all once through, don't stunt your spiritual growth and maturity in Christ by not continuing to feed yourself wholesome meals on a regular basis. I recommend that you read other books on Bible study and theology and/or enroll in Bible study classes designed to offer you a greater and deeper relationship with God. You can also let your Spiritual Gourmet Chef serve you the Master Chef's sixty-six meals when you dine on the following:

The Royal Candlelight 5 Book Series by Your Spiritual Gourmet Chef

The Royal Candlelight Culinary Book Series offers you five "Spiritual Recipe Books" to help you become a healthy eater of God's Word. Work on your spiritual culinary skills by taking the opportunity to dine with us on all sixty-six books of the Bible under the Royal Candlelight. The Royal Candlelight Recipe Books are prepared as four-course meals fit for royalty, using workbook-style, highly personalized "recipes." All five spiritual culinary recipe books are structured to bring every prince and princess in the royal family of God to a higher standard of godly living. Listed here for your enjoyment of God's fantastic meals is a brief description of each follow-up spiritual recipe book (study guides) written for godly living.

30 Minute Meals With God offers you guidance into a higher form of a godly "rich and royal" life. The Master Chef, Jesus Christ said in John 4:32, "I have food to eat that you do not know about." Here's your opportunity to get into this devotional cookbook, so you can begin to live a meaningful and abundant life, full of love, joy, peace, and prosperity according to God's standards as you dine on the Master Chef, Jesus Christ awesome culinary delicacies found in His Great Recipe Book, The Bible.

The Royal Candlelight and You offers *spiritual gourmet cuisine for the true believer of God.* These recipes consist of upscale "cuisines" selected from the New Testament, focusing on the characteristics and attributes of the Son of God, Jesus Christ. As you dine on these gourmet meals, which have been prepared to teach you in depth about Jesus, you will also learn about His provisions and expectations for every prince and princess in the royal kingdom of God. This book covers the following ten books of the Bible, taken from the New Testament: *Matthew, Mark, Luke, John, Acts, Romans, 1 & 2 Corinthians, Hebrews, and Revelation.*

Dining By Royal Candlelight offers *spiritual fine-dining for the true believer of God.* These in-depth studies cover specially selected books of the Old and New Testaments which consist of one to six chapters each. This spiritual recipe book will teach you the proper etiquette and fine dining techniques required as you dine at the King's banquet table while dining by the true "Royal Candlelight"—the Light of Jesus Christ! This book covers twenty-seven short books of the Bible and will be a good book to start off with if you want to dine on each meal in one sitting. From both the Old and New Testaments, the books covered are:

Ruth, Lamentations, Joel, Obadiah, Jonah, Nahum, Habakkuk, Zephaniah, Haggai, Malachi, Galatians, Ephesians, Philippians, Colossians, 1 & 2 Thessalonians, 1 & 2 Timothy, Titus, Philemon, James, 1 & 2 Peter, 1, 2 & 3 John, and Jude.

The Royal Candlelight Classic Lean Cuisines is full of *spiritually rich lean cuisines for the true worshiper of God.* This is an in-depth study of specially selected books from the Old Testament, offering nonfat recipes covering wisdom and prophesies to help you make wise decisions in your life as you prepare for your new royal lifestyle and what's to come of it. This book covers sixteen books of the Bible from the Old Testament: *Ezra, Esther, Job, Psalms, Proverbs, Ecclesiastes, Song of Solomon, Nehemiah, Isaiah, Jeremiah, Ezekiel, Daniel, Hosea, Amos, Micah, and Zechariah.*

The Royal Candlelight Banquet Feasts is a book of *foundationally rich culinary cuisines for the King's royal children.* These spiritual recipes are in-depth studies of the first thirteen books of the Bible, which includes the foundation of mankind. This ultimate gourmet feast is not a natural taste for everyone, but once you acquire that taste, you'll relish it! It's just a tiny spoonful away from your total spiritual dining enjoyment. This book covers thirteen books of the Bible: *Genesis, Exodus, Leviticus Numbers, Deuteronomy, Joshua, Judges, 1 & 2 Samuel, 1 & 2 Kings, and 1 & 2 Chronicles.*

The Royal Candlelight Recipe Book Series will not only teach you how to study, but will allow you to feast on all sixty-six books of the Bible as you learn. The Royal Candlelight shines brightly from the center of the King's banquet table as these recipes illuminate the importance of dining sufficiently. The Master Chef, Jesus Christ, has prepared this great banquet from the best food to nourish and strengthen every child of God. You will not perish due to your lack of knowledge. You will, however, taste and see that the Lord is truly good—to you and for you!

At the time you read this, all five recipe books may not yet be in print. If you are interested in any of these future publications, please log on to: The Royal Candlelight Christian Publishing Company website at www.royalcandlelight.com and view all of the published books written by your Spiritual Gourmet Chef and other inspiring authors who are spreading the "good news" of the gospel. You can also log on to www.info@royalcandlelight.com and let us know that you want to be put on our company e-mail listing for notification when these recipe books are released for publication.

This 5 book series is a great source of information that will assist you in your studying as you search for the truth. Some of my knowledge on how to study the Bible came from feasting on other theological studies. However, keep in mind that my greatest knowledge first came from studying the Word of God.

Follow us on: Facebook, Twitter and Pinterest

www.ingramcontent.com/pod-product-compliance
Lightning Source LLC
Chambersburg PA
CBHW052001090426
42741CB00008B/1497